Paul Harris

Unconditional Teaching

A ground-breaking journey towards a new style of music teaching

FABER *ff* MUSIC

Dedicated to all teachers who delight in teaching with kindness.

First published by Faber Music Ltd
Bloomsbury House, 74–77 Great Russell Street, London WC1B 3DA
Cover design by Elizabeth Ogden
Page design by Helen Tabor and Sue Clarke
Printed in England by Caligraving Ltd

ISBN10: 0-571-54217-4
EAN13: 978-0-571-54217-8

To buy Faber Music publications or to find out about the full range of titles available please contact your local music retailer or Faber Music sales enquiries:
Faber Music Ltd, Burnt Mill, Elizabeth Way, Harlow CM20 2HX
Tel: +44 (0) 1279 82 89 82
fabermusic.com

Contents

Watch your thoughts, they become your words;
Watch your words, they become your actions;
Watch your actions, they become your habits;
Watch your habits, they become your character;
Watch your character, it becomes your destiny.

老子 Lao Tzu, Mystic Philosopher of Ancient China

Why I wrote this book and some thanks

The concept of unconditional teaching has been floating around in my mind for some time. Its first actual outing in public was in a presentation I delivered at the London Music Education EXPO in early 2020. My wonderful team at Faber Music (many of whom attended) and one or two other friends encouraged me to write about the idea in book form – and so here we are now!

I've always loved both music and teaching – happily two areas of life that few could argue are not of considerable consequence. This book is really about my desire to share these deep enthusiasms and explain the way I think about the wonderful processes of teaching and learning music. Nothing would give me greater pleasure than to feel that all teachers and students are also happy, at ease and taking delight in the process. So I hope you'll enjoy this journey through a little self-reflection, possibly resulting in making a number of sometimes small and maybe sometimes larger adjustments to your approach, in order to make what we do within this treasured profession even more satisfying.

I couldn't have done it without the support and significant help of a number of wonderful friends and fellow musicians and teachers with whom I have discussed the ideas at some considerable length!

So huge thanks to all of them and especially to Bette Gray Fow, Georgina Lee and Harriet Wells who have all spent much time perusing and discussing the text with me in great detail; to Richard Crozier, Simon Dearsley, Pat Hayler, Brian Ley, Dr Maria Luca, Anna Marshall, Peter Noke, Adam Ockelford, Robert Tucker and Dr Caroline Tjoa who have all been very generous with their time and thoughts, and a very special thanks to Emily Bevington, my superb editor at Faber Music, who has spent many hours with these pages. Many thanks also to Dr. Maria Luca and Sir Anthony Selden for their kind and generous words.

This wonderfully comprehensive testament to unconditional teaching informs, invites, stimulates and engages the reader in reflecting on effective teaching by proposing a humanitarian and interactive style that moves beyond personal expectations towards a student-centred approach. Unlike many other books I have read, this is a book with a heart. If you are thinking of becoming a music teacher, or indeed you are already in the heart of the profession, this brilliantly written book, populated with engaging vignettes, invites you to question your personal values and challenge those rigid obstacles that get in the way. Beautifully written, spiced up with psychological ideas and richly illustrated, the book amounts to a concise encyclopedia of developing a more effective teaching approach. It contains insights and useful resources tackling fundamental and interesting questions. In fact, it is an indispensable survival guide for music teachers containing principles that apply to the teaching of any subject. A gem of a book carried through with rigour and love.

Maria Luca, PhD
Head of the Regent's Centre for Relational Studies
and Psychological Well-Being

Foreword

Teaching is one of the most responsible professions on earth. Teachers mould the lives of their students forever. At best, teachers can help develop their students' confidence, help them to think deeply, and encourage them to make the very most of their innate talents. The profession is understandably, if excessively, ringfenced with safety procedures which may discourage the spontaneous, the unusual and the individual. It does not follow, however, that teaching needs to be bland for fear of causing harm.

Paul Harris's book is to be greatly welcomed. Teaching is not like being a doctor, whose task it is to diagnose ailments and then recommend treatments. The risks of missing a condition, misdiagnosing it, or recommending the wrong medicine or treatment could be very serious. The medical profession is rightly hedged by regulations and conditions to help ensure proper procedures are followed. Teaching, in contrast, has much more in common with being a parent than a doctor. Mistakes are rarely life-threatening and thus, teachers can be much more adventurous in their approach, and fuller of joy and spontaneity.

The best teachers in my experience have a deep understanding of the rules but also an inner freedom and confidence to be themselves. They do not abandon their personalities in a jar by their front door when they leave for work in the morning. And their students benefit enormously from being in touch with real human beings, rather than fraught and suppressed ones who are mouthing their words in a way that lacks human warmth.

Paul Harris explores the 'conditions' that can stymie the free flow of a teacher's personality and individuality. He first examines the terminology of 'unconditional teaching' and looks at the purpose of lessons, before reconsidering the conditions that can define them and offering practical ways of navigating them. In the final part of the book, he addresses the teaching methods which can be adopted to achieve unconditional learning, he stimulates self-reflection and offers encouragement to teachers who want to pursue this approach.

The best books about teaching are those that challenge and provoke the reader into reflecting on what they are doing and open up new ways of thinking and being. Forty years ago, when I was studying to be a teacher, I wrote my thesis about the 'unreflective practitioner' – I wish I had access to Paul Harris's book at that time. It would've made me a much better teacher.

Sir Anthony Seldon
Former Vice-Chancellor of The University of Buckingham,
Educator and Contemporary Historian

1 A moment for reflection

We can all become exceptional teachers.

And if that *is* our aspiration – and it is one of the greatest aspirations for any human being – it is helpful if we satisfy certain requirements, or **conditions**.

Hold on! you might be thinking, that seems ironic for the start of a book entitled *Unconditional Teaching* ...

Human minds are filled with a whole host of thoughts, which of course we acquire and assimilate over time. Some of these thoughts will become the (often deep rooted) beliefs and values we hold. Subconsciously, some of these beliefs and values may manifest themselves as conditions that can either help or hinder our teaching.

Much of this book is concerned with how we consider, manage and become aware of these particular thoughts. Especially if we find that they do exist as conditions that may be blocking the flow of effective teaching and learning.

On the other hand, some of the beliefs we may hold can constitute a strong foundation upon which the very best teaching is built:

- The belief that **teaching is an important and unique occupation** and the deeper understanding that just because we can *do* something well (for example, play the piano), doesn't mean we can *teach* it well.
- The belief that **the art and craft of teaching is something worthy of continual further study**. Of course, many people do have an instinct that leads them naturally to good teaching but, through their integrity and desire to do the very best possible, good teachers are constantly driven by an aspiration to *think* and *reflect* continually and more deeply about their teaching.
- The belief in ***what* we are teaching**, in this case music and, more specifically, musical performance within a rich environment of real understanding. And the belief that it can truly contribute to a greater good.
- Finally, the belief that **all those who we are teaching are worthy of our teaching**. If a student turns up for a lesson, then they are worthy to be taught.

If we do satisfy these beliefs (in a sense background requirements or conditions), we open the way for the most exciting and effective teaching and learning. We will be able to embark on a journey that will hopefully take us to a place where our teaching can always flow without interruption, where the process is always positive and engaging, and to an environment where all our students are given the very best chance to succeed.

2 A few words about some words

To make sense of this book, and to avoid any confusion, it is essential that we agree over the meaning of certain key words that lie at the heart of the concept. The most important is of course the word **condition** itself. Interestingly, it is a word with a spectacular number of meanings; here are just a few:

- The state in which you might find something; the *condition* in which you find this book, for example, or in broader terms: '*What is the condition of our education system at the moment?*'
- The situation in which we live or work or find ourselves; '*My working conditions are very good,*' or '*In these icy conditions you'll need to dress warmly.*'
- All the factors that affect the way something happens; '*Under these conditions I'm happy to read on,*' or '*We'll give you a loan on the condition that you provide proof of income.*'
- Medical states: '*Though he suffers from a serious condition, his condition has improved.*'
- A state of physical fitness: '*I'm exercising a lot to get back into condition.*'
- '*For Terms and Conditions tick here*' – in this case we mean the rules which govern our use of particular services.
- And there are yet more: *air conditioning*; *hair conditioner*; the list goes on ...

For the purposes of this book, the word condition will refer to **requirements**:[1]

These are my *conditions*

These are my *requirements*

I'll do this on *condition* that

I'll do this if you meet my *requirements*

If my *conditions* (my *requirements*) are met, then I'm happy and we can move on.

[1] Which is really its original meaning, deriving via the old French *condicion* from the Latin *condicio* meaning stipulation. Looking even further into the past, both the words 'condition' and 'teach' derive from the same Indo-European root: 'deik' meaning to show or to point out. Fascinating!

Here are three other connected words that may also need clarification:

- **Expect** or **expectations:** this is what I assume will happen; the word is also used by some in a stronger, more demanding way: 'This is what I expect from you,' suggesting: 'This is what I want from you in no uncertain terms.'
- **Intentions**: my aims, goals and objectives.
- **Preferences**: the things I like better.

Spoiler alert

Without entirely giving the game away, we will discover that life is pretty much dependent upon conditions, we can't survive without them. So, the fact is, we can never teach absolutely unconditionally, that is, without any requirements. Of course, our students may have conditions (requirements) too, which may play a part in the development of the teacher-student relationship and the effectiveness and enjoyment of the lessons.[2]

[2] See Chapter 9 where the learner's conditions are explored in more detail.

However, we will discover that there may be quite a number of these conditions (which may well be deeply hidden in our subconscious) that might get in the way and block the flow of effective teaching and learning. The purpose of this book therefore is to identify and discover to what extent our teaching might be influenced by those conditions and attempt to find ways of managing, or even eliminating, them.

3 What does it mean to be unconditional?

A parent's love for their new baby is unconditional[3]

Doctors are called to be unconditional in the care they give

Being unconditional suggests that we accept the situation in which we find ourselves and work within it as positively and effectively as possible.

So, should teaching be unconditional? Don't we in fact *need* conditions? Wouldn't life become unmanageable without them?

Why we *do* need conditions

In many aspects of life conditions are essential, and they come in many shapes and sizes.

They may come in the form of **barriers** or boundaries for purposes of protection and to ensure safety. For example:

Or, *'We can have a lesson in this room provided there is nothing in it that will cause physical harm.'*

[3] Musically speaking, singing a lullaby, for example, is unconditional: no one minds (or checks) if the mother is in tune, or singing quite the right rhythm, yet the effect is universal: the child settles down to sleep.

Many **laws** and regulations are, in a sense, simply conditions designed to protect society. For example, we must keep to our side of the road when driving.

Conditions can come in the form of **prerequisites**: *'We'll let you into our college on the condition that you pass our entrance test, and we'll let you stay if you then continue to meet all our conditions, both behavioural and academic.'* College teachers are bound by these conditions, too. They are also bound by other conditions: *'We'll allow you to be a member of staff if you deliver an appropriate quality of teaching.'*

Some conditions are **practical**: for example, in the world of computing conditions form basic operational protocols – the computer won't go to sleep on the condition it is being used.

Some conditions are like **currency**: *'I'll give you a lesson on the condition that you give me an appropriate amount of money for doing so.'* And sometimes conditions form the basis of more transactional human behaviour: *'I'll do this if you do that'*; *'I'll be nice to you if you're nice to me.'*

Some conditions are **unstated** but understood – that's how so much in our world works. Maybe these are implicit conditions; we may not necessarily think of them as conditions, but they still exist: students can come on my *Improve your scales!* course for pianists, preferably on the multiple conditions that they play the piano, have a piano, play scales already and want to improve them.

Here are some more **unstated** (implicit) conditions; they just 'are':

- *'I'll teach you on the condition that you turn up for the lesson.'*
- *'I'll teach you if you have access to an instrument.'*
- *'I'll give feedback on the condition that you do something requiring feedback.'*
- *'I'll teach online as long as we both have a computer, there's a signal and I can hear you.'*

So, conditions are indeed necessary. In fact, as human beings we are to a significant extent 'wired' for conditional behaviour. And the essence of this conditional behaviour is *'I'll do this if ...'* and then we impose requirements, which may be the result of deliberation or derive from deep beliefs or instincts, that we may have never considered. This means, in fact, that most things in life *are* subject to conditions. In teaching, they may play a very big role both in the way we teach and in the way we interact with our students.

Maybe some of our conditions, whether deliberate or not, are in fact blocking the flow of effective teaching and learning. We need to know if they *are* getting in the way and potentially slowing down or even preventing progress. This means we need to know how to recognise our conscious and subconscious conditions, and then learn how to manage them effectively.

'I'll do it on the condition that you understand my conditions'

As we've seen, much of the goings on in life depend upon conditions – we can't escape them. Some are externally imposed, for example, the rules and regulations of teaching institutions or exam syllabuses, and some are self-imposed, for example: *'I'm happy to teach you on the condition that I feel the room is warm enough.'*

For the purposes of this book, I'd like to separate these conditions into two categories: **passive** and **active**. In the first category are all the unstated conditions. These are necessary conditions that simply 'are' and allow things to happen – those we are unlikely to want or need to change (some examples are listed in the previous section of this chapter). These I will now call **passive** conditions and are not especially pertinent to our discussion.

Then there are all the conditions (or requirements) that we actually have the potential to control. These I shall call **active** conditions. Whilst some might be helpful, many end up as *negative* forces that can ultimately block flow, that can get in the way, that can restrict or stop things from happening. For example, the more unrealistic conditions some teachers may have that end up being unsatisfied or unfulfilled and so disappoint, maybe even annoy: an example of this would be a teacher expecting students to practise for (an unrealistic) amount of time or to progress at a particular pace. It is active conditions which largely inform our approach to teaching, and so are the primary focus of this book.

An unconditional approach to teaching

For most of us, it's our worthy intentions – our aims, targets or objectives – that drive us forward. To realise these intentions, we need to avoid conditions that might get in the way. If our intention is to help our students be in a better place at the end of a lesson than they were at the start, then working towards being more unconditional in our approach may play a vital part.

Being truly unconditional in our teaching and in our relationships with our students (maybe in our lives in general) would ultimately mean giving without necessarily requiring anything to be done in exchange. Therefore, we can never be entirely unconditional. Mostly, we are detached from the passive conditions (which we probably rarely think about) but need to be aware of the active ones that may be problematic and negative (which we shall shortly explore in detail), allowing us to control and then maybe to eliminate them. In this way, by moving towards a more unconditional environment, where the emphasis is on delight and fostering the student's pleasure in the process of learning music, we can aspire to do our best whatever the circumstances.

4 What are our own conditions?

We all have conditions – probably many – and we've most likely never really thought much about them. Maybe we've simply intuitively inherited these conditions from our own teachers. The important question is what effect these conditions might have on our teaching. And if the effects are negative, we need to be particularly aware of them.

Before reading on, spend a few minutes reflecting on whether you can identify ***your* conditions**, in other words your requirements as a teacher. Perhaps write them down.

As you begin to do so, you may be surprised to find you have quite a number! Many obvious ones (from the passive category) you can put aside. If we're giving an instrumental lesson, for example, it's helpful that we have a student and they have an instrument in reasonable working order. Conditions that promote pupil care and safety also need not be noted: for example, *'I'll teach you this song on the condition that it's not going to damage your voice.'*

We're on the search for the conditions or requirements that are to be found more deeply in our subconscious, the conditions that may be loaded with underlying biases, preconceptions and psychological issues which may affect our teaching or demotivate our students.

In the list that follows, you may feel that some of the conditions are not really conditions at all, rather they are situations that we must live with and to which we respond in natural and instinctive ways. But if these situations, which can become conditions, have the effect of irritating us, even to a small degree, and the quality of our teaching is negatively affected, it becomes essential to develop our awareness of them and consider more effective ways to manage them. On the surface, many of them look innocuous enough, but in scrutinising them more deeply (which we shall do in Chapter 6), we may find they are not as innocent as they seem.

As you read through the list (which isn't in any order of importance), don't feel there is any finger pointing going on. Read with an open mind and don't worry if you recognise some of the conditions in your own teaching. If you do feel a particular condition is one that you might impose on your students (or yourself) – knowingly or not – that is okay. This is a first step towards explaining, understanding and then managing that condition more positively and dealing with it more effectively – and by doing so, ultimately helping us to improve our teaching.

Each condition should begin with the following thought:

> *I prefer it, and will be more comfortable in my teaching, on the condition that ...*

... the teaching room is nice

I've taught (and have been taught) in a cupboard (albeit a large one!), in a corridor (with constant interruptions) and sundry other less than ideal spaces. If you've taught in institutions such as schools or colleges, the chances are you will have done so too. To what extent might the space in which we find ourselves influence our mood and so, perhaps, our teaching? Can the space in which we teach become a condition?

... the student is respectful

What if our student seems to lack appropriate respect for us as a teacher? How does that make us feel? Will that student get the best from us if we feel disrespected? Do we *expect* our student to show appropriate respect, and if they don't, can that then become a condition?

... the student has practised

The deal is, *'I'll be happy to teach you but you have to practise.'* Is practice a deal-breaker? Do you feel there's not much point in putting in the teaching effort if the student hasn't practised? Is it another example of a lack of respect? How much might this affect your attitude towards the student? Does it therefore become another condition?

... the student has all their books with them

Can students expect us to serve up an effective lesson if they have left their books at home? Or, in online lessons, the books 'fell behind the piano'. Is this another example of disrespect, of not really caring? If they have forgotten (or lost) their books, might it affect our mood? Does it become a condition?

... the student makes mistakes

I sometimes hear the view that if students didn't make mistakes, there wouldn't be much point in having a lesson – this then renders the making of mistakes a condition.

... the student is attentive and cooperative

Of course, it's nice when our students behave well and do what we tell them – but sometimes this might not quite happen as we wish. And if it doesn't happen, we understandably might become irritated, maybe even annoyed or bad-tempered. *'I'll teach you if you're attentive and cooperative,'* – it sounds a reasonable condition.

... the student is interested

If our students are interested in what we're teaching them then that certainly makes life a lot easier. What if our student doesn't respond with the enthusiasm we were expecting? If they're not interested, might our inclination to teach them with any energy or dedication be understandably less strong? It is not uncommon for students to come for lessons at the behest of a parent so causing their particular levels of interest and enthusiasm to be lower than we might like. Does this become a condition? And what control do we have over this?

... the student tries hard

'I'll try hard if you try hard.' This also seems a reasonable condition. If our student seems to be acting in a lazy fashion, not really putting in appropriate effort, could it become a point of contention?

... the student rises to our expectations

'I'm the kind of teacher who has high expectations and this student is not rising to them.' How might we feel under such circumstances? *'I'll teach you ... '* or maybe, *'I'll teach you with more energy and purpose ... if you're always trying to rise to my expectations.'* It becomes another condition.

... the student's general needs relate to my abilities, specialism, tastes and preferences

It seems a reasonable condition. If someone asked me to teach them to fly a plane, I would suggest they look elsewhere and find an expert in that field. But the condition becomes a little more complex if perhaps you are a classical guitarist, and a student wants to learn pop or jazz guitar.

... the student is progressing

If a particular student seems to be progressing at a faster pace than others, might we, subconsciously invest more care and energy in that student? If so, might the progress rate of a student (in relation either to a defined or undefined curriculum) be yet another condition we are unconsciously applying to the situation?

... the student can do it

For school-age students, situations may arise where a teacher feels a student wouldn't be able to play the piece the student wishes to learn. Maybe the student wants to learn an arrangement of a pop song but the teacher is aware, through experience, that trying to teach it is often unsuccessful, owing to its rhythmic and technical complexities. *'I'll teach it on the condition I feel you have the ability to learn it'* does seem a reasonable condition. Adult learners often wish to play music beyond (sometimes way beyond) their technical level. How might we manage this condition which otherwise might cause a certain level of tension and frustration?

... the student is not better than me[4]

If the student is 'better' than the teacher, doesn't this mean that there is not much that can be done for that student by that teacher, and wouldn't it put that teacher in a rather uncomfortable and untenable situation? Surely being more advanced than our student is a necessary condition?

[4] I've always had a problem with the word 'better' in this context – for example, one student is not *better* than another – maybe just more advanced in some aspects. Similarly, I don't believe in the easy/difficult concept when it comes to education: it's not *difficult* to do something if we know how to do it. It is much more helpful and logical to think the route as being from simple to more complex.

'Hidden' conditions

There are a number of what we might call 'hidden' conditions, conditions that are possibly formed from even deeper beliefs and values. Conditions that, surprisingly, may be responsible for much of what we think, and consequently the way we behave and interact with our students, without us ever having really considered them.

Do you believe, for example, that some people are more innately musical than others? It is a complex and multi-faceted question. There is clearly no simple yes or no answer (and to go into a sufficiently well-argued and necessarily philosophical and developmental discussion here is probably beyond the scope of this book) but it can easily become an unspoken condition in our teaching. How might we treat the students perceived to be more innately talented differently to others who don't seem to be?

There are a multitude of other musical attributes that we may feel are important: the ability to sight-read, understand musical theory, play or sing in tune, play or sing in time, a natural desire to build a thorough and wide-ranging technique, an ability to shape a phrase naturally and beautifully, a desire to study a broad range of styles, and so on. If a student doesn't show interest in these areas or can't do them easily, how might it affect our view of that student and so the way that we teach them? Are we less inclined to put in the care and effort for this student compared to a student who does seem to display all or most of those qualities? Under these circumstances each of these attributes (and maybe more) become conditions. Might we, to an extent, be engaging (albeit subconsciously) in favouritism?

Maybe we love Beethoven sonatas. We have two new beginners. The first, in some mystifyingly intuitive way, via something deep inside our minds, we believe one day will probably play one of our beloved Beethoven sonatas. The second, despite being equally as pleasant a student, we somehow believe, deep down, probably never will. This judgment or thought – more an instinct – has materialised in some remote part of our consciousness. Perhaps we feel one of these students (the first) is more 'like us'.[5] We didn't ever *think* the thought in so many words but might this subconscious feeling affect the way we teach the two students?

[5] An example of what is often termed 'unconscious bias'.

The impact of conditions

Two important questions emerge from all of these conditions. The first prompts us to consider how we might feel about investing our time and energy if students don't, to some degree, meet all of these conditions. Might our behaviour be affected too? Subconsciously there are all sorts of ways these conditions might impact on the way we treat our different students:

- We might inadvertently create a less warm environment for those students who don't satisfy our conditions.
- We may not treat those students' responses with the same care and attention they deserve.
- We may give more criticism to students who test our conditions whist giving more positive feedback to the 'better' ones.
- We might give our 'better' students more opportunities to learn new and more interesting material and maybe unconsciously (or maybe intentionally) 'patronise' others by giving them less interesting and challenging repertoire, feeling they won't rise to the challenge.
- We might even be a little less friendly and encouraging to our 'less good' students.

In Chapter 6, we will look at all of these conditions and see how, by considering each from different perspectives, they might cease to be conditions. By recognising our own conditions in our teaching, we can begin to liberate our students from the weight of our unconscious expectations for them.

There are no 'bad' students

The second question that emerges is of paramount importance: can we have good (perhaps better labelled 'worthwhile') students without them having all (or most of) the qualities and abilities listed that we may feel are important? The answer must be a resounding yes.

And the reason is simply because there *are* no bad students[6] – *all* our students are worthwhile. Each student is worth our while teaching them. Each is equally deserving of our best teaching. In my presentations I often ask teachers if they have a 'best' student. Of course, it's human nature to think in these terms – to classify our students in this way. The downside is that if we have a 'best' student we then, through simple logic, probably also have a 'worst' student. The result is that we might then value our 'best' student conditionally (since they meet our conditions) and others, who don't meet our conditions, may suffer as a consequence.

[6] See *The Virtuoso Teacher*, Chapter 4, 'Getting the best out of our pupils' (Faber Music Ltd).

If, on the other hand, we don't have a best (or a worst) student, and instead we just have students, unlabelled and not judged or compared relative to one another, then each is allowed to progress at their own pace and at their own level. When we achieve this, we are on the way to valuing our students unconditionally.[7] And if we value our students unconditionally, we almost can't help teaching unconditionally.

[7] Self-comparison, however, is always to be encouraged: 'How did I do this week compared to last week?'

In some contexts, however, the use of comparison in teaching *is* important and often unavoidable. This is most apparent in the higher levels of education, particularly the STEM disciplines.[8] For example, in the medical world we need to find the most able individuals to perform procedures such as effective brain surgery, and in engineering, we need the individual who can design the most structurally stable bridge. Comparing one with another is often the best way of finding such individuals.

[8] Science, Technology, Engineering and Mathematics. The acronym STEM was adopted by scientists in the National Science Foundation in 2001 to address curriculum choices in schools.

In the musical world, as we approach the higher levels of the pyramid, we are also seeking the most accomplished players and singers to act as inspirations and to sustain musical performance at the most distinguished levels. That being said, as we look to these 'idols', it is crucial to avoid feeling inadequate or discouraged as a result of comparison. Instead, it is always better to view them as aspirational figures. Whilst it is unquestionably good to maintain a healthy and robust desire to advance, simultaneously we must try our best to be satisfied with where we are at any one time. If not, we might set up a potential for stress, perhaps also leading to frustration and unhappiness.

If we find ourselves having to choose a winner in a competition, audition or other award, even though the process *is* comparative, it is important that we acknowledge that on another day, the result could be different. All competitions, exams, auditions and the like are just snapshots of ability at a given moment – a comparative difference between one musician and another is never absolute. We should always strive to be kind, positive and appreciate all contenders.

⁕

Before we look at ways to reinterpret these conditions, let's re-examine the purpose of a lesson – the time in which all of these conditions play out.

5 What are lessons for?

There are of course a number of answers to this question. On a practical level, lessons are (to an extent) a time to pass on information and to introduce and reinforce all kinds of mental, physical and musical social skills; more specifically they can sow the seeds for the development of technique, musicianship, reading music notation, listening, memory and expressive skills. They give students direction and keep them on the right track. They allow students to improve and, of course, lessons can inspire and motivate.

From a slightly different perspective, lessons give our students the opportunity to achieve, to progress, to shine and to do well. They give them the opportunity to communicate – through the music and also through language, both verbally and non-verbally. Lessons also give students the opportunity to smile and to laugh.[9] Smiling and laughing don't preclude hard work and concentration. The teachers I remember best are those who made me smile and laugh. And when we do smile and laugh we learn best, we are more malleable and prepared to change our minds … and we work harder. Any kind of tension (physical or mental), fear, anxiety or general unhappiness is likely to obstruct learning and impair performance; endorphins are not released and the brain simply doesn't absorb.[10]

[9] Occasionally you might meet a student who struggles to smile (for many it's an adolescent thing). This doesn't mean we shouldn't give them every opportunity to do so (maybe they are smiling, but inwardly).

[10] In fact, fear *can* release endorphins – but this is more the kind of fear resulting from a ride on a big dipper or seeing a horror film. Fear encountered in a learning situation is likely to trigger the body's stress response system which can upset the brain's functions and inhibit learning.

At the highest levels, lessons can do still more. Here we are looking at the development of special qualities: self-confidence, self-esteem, self-belief and self-worth. If you research these terms, you will find slightly differing and sometimes overlapping definitions. But there does seem to be a consensus that puts them in a kind of sequential and hierarchical order:

> When the teaching really matches the learning, the result is high-energy and continually positive movement forward, and so we become responsible for helping our students to develop their **self-confidence.** Simultaneously, students are also gaining a sense of control over their learning which helps them develop a much more positive view of themselves. This fuels their **self-esteem** which is really allowing them to see themselves in a good way and reducing their need to compare themselves (often unfavourably) with others. This may take them to the next, and highly significant level, to **self-belief**. With self-belief a student believes in their ability to complete tasks and to achieve their goals. This gives them the strength (the perseverance and resilience) to get on with things in a positive and constructive way.
>
> Self-belief is not arrogance, and it doesn't result in an over-active ego. Unless, occasionally, it is flaunted serving the aim of feeling superior to others. It is a quiet and contained trust that comes from our teacher having a belief in us and causing us to believe in ourselves. And self-belief gives

us, and our students, **self-worth** – maybe the ultimate of these qualities as it further fuels our confidence and provides self-acceptance, an energy to try harder, to have a go, to take part and to contribute positively. It provides security, and when we feel safe, we learn at our best.

Let's look at this concept of *worth* a little more closely. What are the sources of both *our* worth and the worth of our students? The answers may well influence our deeper and more hidden conditions.

Our own personal sense of worth (in the context of our teaching) should be invested in our ability to promote in our students those qualities already listed: appropriate achievement and progress, encouragement to communicate and to smile and laugh; and, on the higher levels, in our ability to nurture their confidence, self-esteem and self-belief.

Our worth, on the other hand, should not be based on the number of our students who might play advanced and more complex pieces, achieve high marks at exams, always play in tune (or in time, or with the most beautifully controlled sound, and so on). Of course, it is nice when these things happen (and we should always aspire towards them) but as teachers they don't define our worth, or shouldn't.[11] If we focus only on those we think of as our 'best students' (our 'more advanced students'), it promotes conditionality in our teaching. We might become exclusive: 'I only teach good students.' Or we might become unhappy, fearing what others might think about us; we might become resentful, frustrated, even angry or jealous: 'I have so many bad students, I don't deserve this.' We begin to move into blame culture – it's someone else's fault – which is never a good thing. If we get into this kind of thinking, it becomes necessary to take a step back and analyse the situation more carefully. Certainly don't take it out on your students!

[11] Potentially this is a real problem for teachers in institutional situations where schools are ranked based on student performance. Students who are underperforming might be set aside in favour of the higher achievers as these individuals may bring more 'positive regard' to the teacher, department or institution. Happily this is not a problem in individual or small group music teaching.

Our view of our students' worth (again in the context of learning) should be dependent upon their *achievement*: what have they achieved since the beginning of the lesson or since the last lesson, or in relation to their starting point? It shouldn't be dependent on their *attainment*: passing exams, for example. For every human being is different, learning and processing at different speeds – often significantly so. If every little thing done successfully, and with some degree of effort or maybe courage, is acknowledged and applauded, then our students begin to develop a strong sense of self-worth.

⁂

Now, with these thoughts on the reasons for having lessons in mind, let's look at those conditions described in Chapter 4 again and see whether we can find a new way forward, a new mindset, where the conditions might cease to be conditions. We can begin to create a more unconditional environment in which to live and work – an environment that promotes more positivity, flow and achievement.

6 Changing our mindsets

In Chapter 4, we looked at many conditions that, one way or another, might affect our mood and expectations, and that may in turn affect the way we teach. Let's look at each one and see whether we might be able to find a different approach, an approach which will help to change their status as conditions.

Remember to preface each with:

> *I prefer it, and will be more comfortable in my teaching, on the condition that ...*

... the teaching room is nice

Maybe, if we're teaching in an institution, we *are* given a less than pleasant space in which to teach. *I deserve better* may be the thought that instinctively comes to mind. *How can I teach in all this mess?* When possible, try to speak to someone in authority and try not to pass any frustration onto your students. It's nice to teach in a nice room, but does it in fact really matter? I had many of my music lessons when I was at school in an enlarged cupboard (of course it wouldn't be allowed today) but it didn't seem to worry my teacher and it certainly didn't worry me. In the direst of circumstances we can try to take some responsibility for the room and do our best to make it as pleasant as possible.[12] Can we improve the room in some small ways? On many occasions I have tidied up a little before the first student arrives. Or alternatively, we can just ignore it and carry on. Consciously make the decision that it's simply not going to trouble you. We have removed it from being a condition. If we don't, that annoyance is likely to make its way, somehow, into the lesson. And of course, the whole point of the lesson is to be deeply involved in music – something we love, and so, through this immersion in the joy of teaching and learning, entirely transcends the space. A friend of mine calls her teaching room her sacred space – a space that somehow exudes safety and calmness, where students can relax and feel happy to do their best. It has become an unconditional space.

[12] There are certain cases where teaching can't take place; if the temperature is below any prescribed legal limit, for example, or there is anything in the space that might give rise to physical injury.

... the student is respectful

What about dealing with a seemingly disrespectful student? Might we consider a student who seems disengaged or very low energy disrespectful? Is that student likely to get the best from us?

If we are experiencing blatant rudeness or antagonism that is another matter and will naturally need dealing with in an appropriate way. Notify a parent, or a senior teacher or administrator if it occurs in an institution. Happily that kind of disrespect is rare in individual or small group music teaching.

People, in the end, usually mirror each other's behaviour. Difficult though it might be on occasion, if we are always respectful *to* our students, even to our apparently disrespectful ones, they may well eventually change their behaviour. So how can we achieve this?

I'd like to introduce you at this point to Carl Rogers, a very influential and distinguished American psychologist who developed the idea of Unconditional Positive Regard.[13] Rogers was responsible for training therapists, often those dealing with very troubled patients. Hopefully most of our students will not be so troubled, and, often, we may never get to know what may be behind their behaviour, but by showing them Unconditional Positive Regard they may soon change that behaviour. There are a number of ways we can do this – none of them requiring any psychological training!

[13] For more on Unconditional Positive Regard, see Carl Rogers' *On Becoming a Person: A Therapist's View of Psychotherapy* (Constable, 2004).

First of all, try always to acknowledge any successes and achievements – however small. In the proactive Simultaneous Learning approach,[14] where lessons unfold as a series of logical and sequential activities, each activity should be able to be deemed a success.

[14] See *Simultaneous Learning* (Faber Music Ltd).

▼

Second, take time to explain the reasoning behind instructions: this is why we're doing this; this is why we're making this particular connection. On occasion, ask your student why they think you set up the next activity in the way that you did.

▼

And third, have in mind the fact that the teaching is always directed towards the student eventually becoming independent. Shortcuts, which may allow a student to do something more quickly, but without really understanding how, are not always such a good idea. They can also cause the student who may revel in challenging authority to rebel against what they see as unexplained 'instructions', and so feel disrespected by the teacher. Ultimately, shortcuts won't contribute to the journey towards independence.

Above all this, if we believe the best of someone, we are more likely to get the best back.

We can also demonstrate respect for our student by what is sometimes termed the currency of gratitude. Fred De Witt Van Amburgh,[15] wrote:

[15] An American writer and publisher (1866-1944) who wrote a number of motivational books.

'Gratitude is a currency that we can mint for ourselves and spend without fear of bankruptcy.'

A typical lesson will see, many times over, the teacher asking their student to carry out an activity which the student usually then does – would it not then be nice to thank them? Of course, we couldn't possibly thank them *in words* every time this happens.[16] But a *feeling* of gratitude might always be present, maybe conveyed by a simple smile or other affirmative non-verbal gesture, or an enthusiasm in our tone of voice. And, if we have given our student an appropriate task, one they understand and can see its underlying

[16] Though the frequent use of phrases like 'well done', 'we're getting there', 'that made my day', 'you've come a long way on that piece' are all very welcome.

logic, they similarly thank *us*. Again, it's a feeling, never spoken. Two parties thanking each other. Silently. It's currency. It buys us more hard work, more engagement, it engenders mutual respect. It makes us feel happier and builds better relationships.

Together these approaches will earn us our students' respect. There are, on the other hand, some teachers who don't believe that respect should have to be earned. They feel they are entitled to that respect as a matter of course. Maybe it is a point of view worth re-examining.

Sometimes a student may seem disrespectful or sulky if they are struggling to understand the words, vocabulary or concepts we are using.

'A giraffe is high, why is my teacher calling this note high?'

If each new word (a new technical term, for example) is introduced carefully (the meaning reinforced when necessary) and appropriate connections made, it can be surprising what effect that might have.

Of course, there may be, in extreme cases, a personality clash with a particular student; that clash may be due to factors we may never know and not connect with our work – but we do need to acknowledge this possibility. Furthermore, for whatever reason, and however hard we try, the student remains difficult. Sometimes a change of teacher might be the ultimate solution. However, this should only be a last resort.

Most students are of course respectful, though occasionally we might receive what we interpret as disrespect when none was intended. Extreme shyness may, for example, result in disconnected, unenthusiastic, or even abrasive behaviour. But if we accept that having respectful students is not always simply an entitlement, that we have some responsibility in the matter, then it ceases to be a condition and an obstruction to effective teaching and learning.

... the student has practised

How might we react if our student hasn't practised? Get annoyed? Get frustrated? Send the student away? Or take responsibility? Ideally we should aim to teach in such a way that students go home thinking, *I want to do some practice.*

A lesson is a series of transactions, and they occur along this pattern:

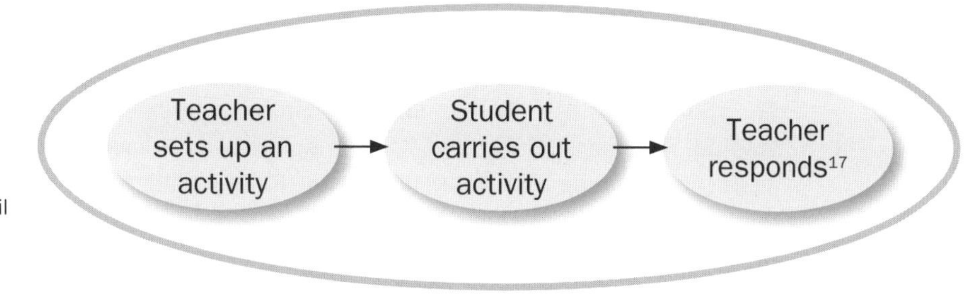

[17] This subject, in particular a discussion of different types of feedback, is considered in detail in *The Virtuoso Teacher* (Faber Music Ltd).

If we adopt certain strategies in our response, then it is more likely that our student *will* do some practice:

- Aim to make each of our responses as positive as possible. There is almost never any need to respond negatively. Such responses are ultimately toxic.
- Sometimes, begin our responses with, *'When you practise this ...'* – we are not *telling* our student to practise, just assuming they will.
- Occasionally during the lesson ask, '*What shall we do next?*' and also, '*When practising this, what might you do next?*'[18]

[18] It may be helpful for students to have a copy of my *Simultaneous Learning Musical Map of the World* to refer to during their practice to help them decide what to do next. Many teachers have one in sight in the lesson too. These can be downloaded from my website: *paulharristeaching.co.uk*

We can't make our students practise. If we try to force them, they may become resentful and may eventually give up. Our job is to entice them into doing some practice simply because they want to.

Even if they haven't practised, we can still give an effective, useful and enjoyable lesson. Avoiding any unkind comments, and within the Simultaneous Learning approach, we simply move forward on whatever music our students are studying, using appropriate ingredients to explore and experiment and making connections (maybe with scales, theory, aural, improvisation, or other repertoire) and always acknowledging effort and achievement, however small.

Through this approach we can eliminate practice as a restrictive condition.

... the student has all their books with them

Students do sometimes forget their books (a situation that is more unlikely to occur if teaching online! Though they may still have 'got lost' or 'dropped behind the piano'). It's useful to try to work out why a student might arrive without their music books (especially if this becomes persistent). It could be the consequence of how the last lesson ended. If, for some reason, that lesson finished on a slightly sour note (we hope this never happens, but realistically, it might occasionally) then forgetting the books may be a (subconscious) form of withholding.

If the student hasn't practised and (understandably) feels their teacher will be annoyed (because their teacher usually is) then forgetting the books gives them an excuse: 'You won't be able to get more annoyed with me because I don't have the music to illustrate further that I haven't practised ...' They could also be trying to tell us that they don't like the particular pieces that they're learning.

Don't let arriving without music books become a condition. Instead, we need to be imaginative and resourceful – there are so many things we can do without the books. Learning more ingredients (from pieces or songs currently being studied), improvising around those ingredients, making connections (and indeed connecting with less frequently visited places like perhaps theory), refining technique, playing duets, and so on.

Maybe they just forgot their books – it's not that important.

... the student makes mistakes

'If my student didn't make mistakes there would be no point in lessons ...' – it is certainly a point of view. However – and this may be a slightly controversial question to consider – whose responsibility is it if our student does make a mistake? If we set up each activity in the lesson carefully; making sure our student *really* knows what they are expected to do next and are confident in having a go, then the chances for mistakes are hugely reduced. It is our responsibility to set that up. Students may make (let's call them) slips – many slips maybe. And if on the journey to 'getting' it, they make a slip – that's fine. They know what they are aiming towards. Slips are not mistakes. There are many understandable and even interesting 'slips' on the way to success. We learn from them. There is no emotional value attached to making a slip.

On the other hand, mistakes can be toxic when made because students are confused, don't understand something, or don't sufficiently know what is expected of them.

> Teach students the difference between a mistake and a slip; and refer to slips as and when appropriate. If you prefer the word 'mistake', make it clear that the word is not loaded with any negativity. If mistakes have negative consequences, the resulting fear can block a student's motivation and belief in themselves.

I know of some teachers who seem to relish their students making mistakes in order that they might exert their ego and authority over them. Such teachers might take a moment to reconsider this viewpoint.

We also need to consider the 'reacting to mistakes' kind of teaching where students so often end up giving up. Unlike Simultaneous Learning, here the approach is basically: student plays and teacher reacts to what was offered, usually meaning the correcting of mistakes. Ultimately this is an exclusive kind of teaching that only a minority manage to see through. The majority give up having been given the impression that they really aren't very good. It's sad to think how many would-be musicians have probably been lost to this kind of teaching over the years. I don't object to this kind of teaching and, if done sensitively, it can be useful at times. It may be helpful to see it on a continuum – the most severe kind of reactive teaching on one end and the most creative kind of Simultaneous Learning on the other:

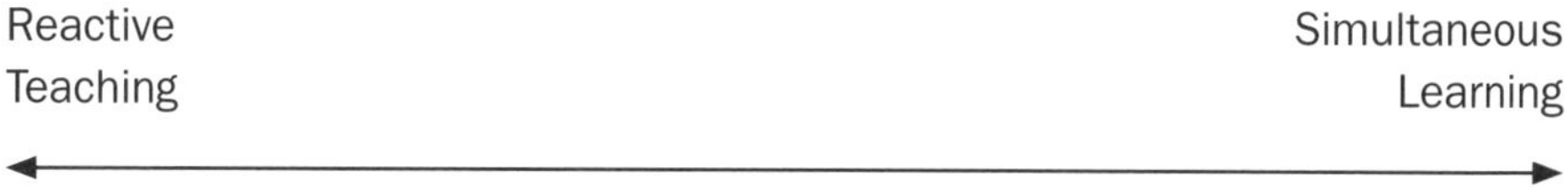

Reactive Teaching ◄——————————————————► Simultaneous Learning

... the student is attentive and cooperative

These qualities will grow from the type of teaching that reduces mistake making. The Simultaneous Learning approach, where each activity is set up carefully, ensuring that ingredients are all understood resulting in relatively constant achievement will certainly help. Students will feel safe and comfortable and so, in most cases, will be attentive and do what you want them to. Furthermore, if they are engaged and are enjoying the process, if they know you are on their side wanting their best, if they know you believe in them and if they believe that they can meet the demands of a task, they are more likely to be even more attentive and cooperative – and happy and content. Through nurturing this positive environment, we are also setting up the potential for students to explore and experiment on their own, which will also further improve their desire to practise.

... the student is interested

Of course, many students *are* naturally interested (often deeply interested) in what we are teaching them. And again, maybe for our slightly less naturally interested students, it will develop as a consequence of our own enthusiasm for the subject. Though maybe some students' particular interests will still be slightly restricted – they may be happy to learn pieces or songs, but not to sight-read or play scales or connect with theory, for example. Here we can employ our more magical powers – the subtle art of subterfuge!

'What a lovely phrase that is – and you played it very well. It seems to be based on a pattern [pointing at a scale in the music] – let's explore the pattern in a bit more detail ...'

▼

'Here's a similar pattern, can you play it without preparation?'

▼

'Here's the same phrase in another key, what key might that be? Let's explore that pattern before we play it ...'

▼

'Here's a pattern, but it's a little different; let's see if we can detect what the differences are ...' and so on.

And in that little learning journey we have made connections to scales, sight-reading and theory. All quite gently and without giving any labels.[19] Maybe we introduce the labels next lesson. In time, with some patience, and a bit of imagination and resourcefulness, we should be able to develop our students' interest in all sorts of directions.

[19] In fact, we can often delay labelling until ideas are well embedded.

Sometimes a student may have what we might consider such a narrow interest that the thought of teaching them (for more than a few lessons anyway) becomes quite a challenge. A friend of mine had a student who only wanted to learn pieces by Bartók. And the student was pretty determined to stick to this very restricted musical diet. The repertoire had become a condition in the mind of the student: *'I'll carry on learning the piano on the condition that you teach me music by Bartók.'* The teacher respected this desire for quite a while and then gradually introduced some pieces that were similar but could gently steer the student in other directions. Once that trust and respect were well established, the student became open to suggestion and the courage and desire to explore outside the condition was enabled.

In this case, conditions in the minds of both the teacher *and* the student were managed and overcome.

And as for students who are there, initially anyway, as a result of parental desire, with a little careful nurturing and inventiveness, we may be able to capture their imaginations too.[20]

[20] In my case, it was entirely my mother's decision that I would start music lessons and it was she who chose the clarinet. I didn't really know what a clarinet was and can remember my disappointment at it not living in a very large and long case that I could proudly show off during my journeys to school on the London Underground. But I'm very glad she did make that decision, and my first teacher certainly did all the right things.

... the student tries hard

Given everything we've discussed so far – if our student is feeling safe, has a healthy degree of confidence and self-worth and so is likely to believe they can do what you ask of them – then they *will* try hard. They may even take risks and try even harder! There's no emotional penalty to pay if things don't go quite right. Your student has learnt to trust you. Rather than *'I won't teach you unless you try hard,'* let's set up the situation so that your student wants to try hard. It's no longer a condition, it's simply become part of the natural flow. Again, this will have a further impact on a student's practice (they may begin to explore more on their own) as well as contributing to success in many other life-spheres too.

... the student rises to our expectations

First of all, we need a clear understanding of **expectation** within the context of conditions. It's a word on a continuum:

Realistic Expectations	◄────────►	Unrealistic Expectations
Unconditional Teaching		*Conditional Teaching*

At one end, our expectations are realistic, given the known information. For example:

'I know this student has a number of important commitments this week, so I don't expect them to do as much practice as usual.'

And so, giving an effective lesson is not conditional on whether the student has practised or not.

Moving along the spectrum, expectations gradually become more unrealistic:

> 'Even though I know this student has a number of important commitments this week, I still expect them to practise for at least three hours every day.'

Now our expectation has become a condition which, if not satisfied, may give rise to all sorts of negative behaviours. When expectations become unrealistic, they become conditional. Ultimately, they can reach the point at which they may begin to crush motivation and creativity and replace it with a negative atmosphere of extreme pressure. This kind of behaviour is unlikely to end happily.

Expectations simply need to be realistic and if realistic expectations are exceeded, both student and teacher can feel particularly pleased.

High expectations are also fine as long as they are *realistically* high and appropriate, and the teacher creates a secure environment in which their students can aspire to them safely and confidently. If a teacher knows a student to be of high mental resilience, then presenting them with challenges is, of course, quite acceptable. But high expectations have a darker side.

> 'I'm hard to please ... I'm never satisfied with anything short of perfection.'

If these (usually high) expectations are in fact unrealistic we are now into conditional and highly judgemental thinking and teaching. In extreme cases, this attitude can become very intimidating and block the flow of learning.

Needs versus expectations

Instead of having unrealistic (or even, sometimes, realistic) expectations, let's think more in terms of our students' *needs*. Rather than seeing our students' success in terms of meeting our expectations, let's see it in terms of encouraging students to meet *their* needs. This requires us to have good reserves of empathy – the ability to connect with others and understand them and, as teachers, to help students understand themselves.[21]

[21] *See also page 62.*

Often teachers have an agenda: 'This is how I teach this – my good students get it, and my poor students don't.' This exclusive and conditional approach, the opposite of inclusive teaching, does nothing to build the self-worth of the majority of students. In fact, it is based on a form of intentional natural selection which destines many to failure. In other words, those who don't meet the hypothetical 'cut' fail virtually before they've even begun. And will almost certainly give up sooner rather than later. We really want to avoid that.

Instead, we should always be searching for what each student needs to do next in response to *how* they just did *what* they just did – not based on a mythical 'perfect student' or a rigid preordained order of progression. The effective teacher is always resourceful and has many imaginative strategies to call upon in order to respond in the best way to a particular student in a particular moment.

Our standards and our expectations need to be fluid – always adaptable – and always appropriate to the student. Therefore, if appropriate, allow expectations (whatever they are) to slip a little into the background to make way for our students' needs. This does require a little patience and confidence but is well worth it.

If a teacher's expectations are continually unrealistic and students are rarely able to meet them, students will feel that they are constantly letting their teacher down: the result can never be a happy one. And for the teacher, there will be constant frustration.

If our expectations are realistic, and we look to our students' needs, we have removed expectations as conditions.

Managing short-term expectations

We also need to consider short-term expectations: literally what we expect to happen once we have issued an instruction. If that instruction is well set up, is part of a carefully planned series of logical and sequential activities (as per the Simultaneous Learning approach), our expectation of the student (i.e. to respond successfully) should be realistically high. But in the style of teaching where a student is simply asked to do something (often without careful preparation) and then the teacher reacts to whatever the student managed, there is a much greater likelihood of things not going so well ...

If the teacher, based on past experience of a student, for example, was expecting a certain response (they've done it well before; they were supposed to have practised it; the teacher simply assumed they would get it right) and it didn't happen, there is room for some block to the flow. The teacher may simply dismiss this attempt (which will, at the very least, have wasted some time) or may get a little frustrated – which is unhelpful for both teacher and student. And if it happens multiple times in a lesson, the frustration, for both student and teacher may well develop and impact significantly on the short- and possibly longer-term. Students' confidence will ebb and the teacher may become increasingly irritated.

By managing our short-term expectations, by removing the possibility of them becoming negative conditions, (*'It'll be a better lesson if you get things right immediately'*), the lesson should flow smoothly.

... the student's general needs relate to my abilities, specialism, tastes and preferences

Here we need to think carefully about who we are, what we do, why we do it and the reasons behind all these considerations.

If a beginner came to me wanting to learn the harp, I would have to say, as a clarinettist, that they would be better with someone who knows how to teach the harp. However, if a student wanted to learn to play jazz or pop – genres maybe outside my expertise, the situation is more complex. I can either say, 'No, I am not able to teach you that, you need to find another teacher who will' or, 'This is not my main area of expertise but I'm happy to have a go and explore this with you.' I know of teachers taking on this challenge and gradually (and maybe a little surreptitiously) introducing music outside the student's preferred genre, with the student gradually enjoying the less familiar with equal satisfaction. We simply need to react honestly, openly and responsibly. We don't have to be fearful of the unknown.

Even if we have a personal dislike of, for example, the work of a specific composer, or sub-genre within our own area of expertise, or there is a particular technique with which we are not comfortable or maybe disapprove of, might we still be happy to try to teach it to our student? Certainly, it should be open to a discussion over how such a task is approached, trying, as we do, to be careful not to let our ego get in the way.[22]

[22] Teaching should always be seen as a self*less* process and never a self*ish* one.

Are we prepared to learn from our students?

> 'Tell me what you know about this music (which I don't know); what are its characteristics? Give me some ideas about how you'd like to move forward with it, what kind of techniques you need to develop, and we'll explore it together.'

We might be prepared to do some homework ourselves and explore areas outside of our own usual specialisms?

... the student is progressing

Virtually all definitions of progress involve movement and change of some kind, and that movement and change will involve some refining of whatever it is we are doing. If we are teaching using the Simultaneous Learning approach – through a series of appropriate, logical and sequential activities, then students are *always* progressing – progressing at *their* speed and *aware* of their progress. If we always deliver the next activity in good spirit, imaginatively, without comparing the sequence or the processing speed with other students, then we will have created energy and flow and our students will always be moving forward and almost certainly always be progressing – so it ceases to be a condition.

... the student can do it

'I'll teach you on condition that you have a reasonable chance of learning this music successfully.' It is a reasonable condition and there are a number of ways it can be managed if it's ever brought into question.

If a student can't do it, there may be a simplified version, for example. Some teachers (*and* students – often adults) are horrified by such a suggestion! But what might be fuelling that horror? It doesn't have to be interpreted as compromising either standards or the sense of musical authenticity or integrity. We mustn't let our ego or our student's ego get in the way. Much better to allow a student the pleasure of making it successfully through simplified arrangements of the 'Moonlight Sonata' or 'Fly Me to the Moon' than either struggle with inadequate control or not play them at all. We could make cuts or edit the music. Maybe we make it a long-term project, identifying all the rhythmical and technical ingredients that have to be mastered, and then developing them carefully and building up the necessary control to take the piece on (before actually taking it on). Or maybe we just have to say, kindly and simply, that this music is too advanced at the moment and we need to develop some particular skills to make learning it worthwhile and achievable. At the same time, reveal a well-considered and engaging route to the intended piece via some other pleasing repertoire.

... the student is not better than me

Though rare, there could be occasions where a teacher might be confronted by a student whom they believe has the potential to match or even exceed their own ability. Some teachers may subconsciously impose their own subset of conditions upon themselves, often driven by the ego ...

> 'If I'm not more advanced than my student I can't teach them because it will demean me and may cost me psychologically.'

Better, and far more constructive, to see this kind of situation as a challenge. Such a situation could potentially cause the teacher to feel insecure and uncomfortable. In most cases, a teacher's security lies in the knowledge that they are (at least) several steps ahead of their student. What should be a joy: 'Haven't I done a great job in sending this wonderful talent out into the world?' becomes fear: 'Everyone will see that I'm not as good as they think I am; I am not as good as I think I am; they will have less respect for me and they will look for a better teacher.' The vanishing 'gap' between the student and teacher may promote feelings of resentment, self-doubt with an attendant loss of self-confidence. This is a situation that sometimes arises more in higher education – maybe the student has a more evolved technique than the teacher, which may also arouse envy.

There is always something that a teacher can offer: the myriad of ideas gained as a consequence of their experience, guidance with phrasing and performance, methods of practice, repertoire suggestions, or knowledge of the industry, for example, or simply moral and psychological support.[23] But if it would be in the student's best interest to recommend they do move on, that course of action could only be seen as responsible, supportive and practical. There is no face to be lost in such a situation. If moving on is not a realistic possibility, at least in the short term, simply offering the student unconditional support is again an entirely honourable way of moving forward.

On the darker side of this situation, I have heard stories of teachers undermining such students by being unnecessarily over-critical, attempting to demoralise them or taking them, needlessly, back to basics to fix a 'problem'.

[23] High-flying music students sometimes have a lot of destructive and counter-productive psychological issues with which the teacher can often help. Child prodigies need particular care as their development will almost certainly not correlate with the norm for their age: relating to others their own age; the stress of living up to expectations and dealing with failure are just some of the issues with which they may need help.

It's always possible to be honest, responsible and considerate, and by doing so, it's not a condition we need ever worry about.

And so to those more hidden conditions ...

The first is connected with the view that some students are more innately musical than others. If we do believe this to be the case, what effect will it have on the way we deal with our students?

Whilst we can all agree that:

- some learners will inevitably make more linear progress than others (maybe moving through the stages of their beginner tutor books with more confidence and speed, or passing more graded exams);
- some learners will acquire more technical proficiency than others;
- some learners will reach greater levels of musical sophistication than others ...

... let's try not to assign a simple scale of value to such achievements. I often ask my students, who may be worrying about the level of their own musicality, to consider the following scenario:

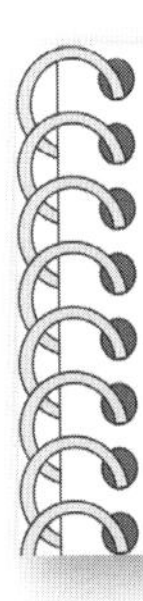

Two players *of the same age* come and play to us. The first player plays a simple piece, which is at their level and they play it beautifully. The second plays a much more complex piece, at *their* level, and it is also beautifully played: who is the more musical? Or are they equally musical in their own ways? Most get the right answer: beautiful playing is beautiful playing.

The problem is that many musicians do hold well-defined views on the subject of relative levels of musicality – and this can inadvertently mean that large numbers of potential musicians are demotivated and put off from pursuing their musical endeavours – even players or singers who have already reached quite advanced standards.

Both perceived levels of musicality and musical potential can become conditions that interfere with progress and enthusiasm. Like everything, the nature and speed of the development of musicality is different from one person to another – often distinctly so: we should *always* try to avoid a one-size-fits-all approach. Maybe for some it's very slow or difficult to see, but it's still there – and it's very important not to discourage or abandon such students.

If we simply change our mindset and value all our students who are doing *their* best at *their* level, then whatever their position on the musical continuum, we always treat them equally. Those conditions which impede progress then no longer exist.

The uplifting story of Derek Paravicini, who was born blind and with severe learning difficulties is a case in point. Through the untiring (and unconditional) efforts of his exceptional teacher, Adam Ockelford, he has become a world renowned pianist. Of course, many will not achieve quite this kind of result, but any result, at any level, is extremely worthwhile.[24]

In my own teaching I've found that some students (especially those who are naturally more subdued) may be shy about displaying or expressing their musicality – even carrying out a simple crescendo may be too much for them. Others may be highly self-conscious in particular areas – singing aloud, for example.[25]

We all have certain boundaries that venturing beyond may cause discomfort. Here, through a growing sense of trust (a result of showing respect for that student, giving lots of appropriate praise and encouragement and leading them on a positive journey) students will learn to feel safe and their musicality will ultimately be revealed.

Sometimes we might get an impression of 'innate musicality' when a student comes from a home where others (siblings or parents) play instruments, or, for example, had a few piano lessons when very young and learned notation, some terminology and a sense of pulse. Maybe this is their second or third instrument. These are all the result of background and experience rather than 'innate musicality'. Of course, it's not really important where these skills came from if the student does have them, but it might affect our judgement one way or another.

As far as that list of musical attributes goes (playing or singing in tune and in time, ability to sight-read, understand theory, and so on), we simply need to think each through carefully and develop a different perspective, in order to eliminate them as conditions. For example, if we set about it systematically enough, with sufficient patience and a belief that it can be taught, all our students can learn to sight-read. We can, with perseverance and determination, teach the student who struggles to play in time or in tune to improve. I've seen many would-be musicians put off because a teacher was too quick to dismiss them for not naturally having these qualities. These musical skills can – like most things – be learned and developed over time, and so ultimately, cease to be conditions.

There remains still a further condition to consider, and it is usually well-hidden. It may be the most significant of all ...

[24] *In the Key of Genius: The Extraordinary Life of Derek Paravicini*, by Adam Ockelford (Arrow, 2008).

[25] Something we need to be particularly aware of in group lessons.

7 'I'll teach you on the condition that you're learning'

'... because if you're not learning, what's the point of my putting in all this effort and giving you lessons?'

This is a condition that can play a major role in a teacher's attitude towards a student; it can have a substantial influence over the way a teacher views that student and ultimately, the way that student is treated.

'I'll teach you, as long as you're learning.'

The interesting question this raises is of course, how do we know whether our student *is* learning? And the associated question, what exactly *are* they learning?

Here are a few questions for you (be honest in your answers!):

- Do your students *always* play their G major scale with the F sharp after you've carefully explained how it comes to be there and reminded them to include it?
- Can they confidently read music that may be significantly simpler compared with pieces or songs they are currently learning?
- Are they happy to rattle off all the scales they've ever learned?
- Can they confidently play or sing all (or most) of the pieces or songs they've ever learned?

If the answer is *not exactly* (and for most of us, if we are being honest, it probably *is*) then we would have to admit that maybe what we have taught has not always been learned. Or what our students have once learned now seems to have been un-learned.

Of course, few of us will probably be able to recall everything we've *ever* learned, and there's nothing wrong or unusual in that. Some things we learn temporarily (verification codes or a route, for example), some things for which we have no longer-term use simply disappear from our memories, some things stay with us always, and other things (with enough effort) might become accessible if we really need to remember them.

But in learning to play an instrument or to sing and to read music, we really need our students to learn (and remember what they've learned), and then gradually build on that learning through effective understanding and making good connections. Otherwise, won't progress be impossible, or at least less likely? Learning to be a musician is, after all, quite a cumulative process.

So it does seem a reasonable condition. *And it is ...*

So how *do* we know if our students are learning? Can we say at what point someone has learned something?

The conventional outward signs of learning are not always dependable. Just because a student may be full of energy, smiling, engaged, motivated and performing well in the short term, doing all we expect, doesn't necessarily mean that they are learning. Just because they are doing it well now doesn't mean they will be able to do it well in five minutes, or when they go home to practise, or next week. These responses don't necessarily indicate that a student is learning. In the same way, if a student appears distracted and maybe seems to be in a low-energy state, it doesn't necessarily mean that they are not learning.

The fact of the matter is that you can't really *see* learning, you can only see the performance – the response after having (apparently) learned something – and that performance may be a poor gauge of how well a student might retain or be able to apply that same knowledge or skill in a different context. Indeed, some students are very good at imitating what they see or hear – often with very little actual *learning* having taken place.

Maybe something was learned: the refinement of a skill or some knowledge, but the control of that refinement was later lost or the knowledge then forgotten. Can we still call it learning? Is there a particular meaningful timescale involved here? Can we be said to have learned something if it only lasts for ten minutes? Do we have to maintain that skill or knowledge for a particular time period (an hour, a week, a year, ten years ...) before we can say it has really been *learned*?

Does it matter?

In a sense it doesn't. As a condition, learning is a complicated one. And our learning (remembering some information or how to do something)[26] is certainly enriched if we see the significance of what we are learning and so *want* to learn it.

Again, its success is very much in the hands of the teacher. If we always teach very carefully, and regularly give our students the chance to prove their learning – to us and to themselves – that learning is likely to be more durable. It becomes less hit and miss ... it becomes less of a condition because we have taken control.

⁂

[26] The idea that learning is remembering goes back to the philosopher, Plato, and in general terms, seems a reliable way to consider the concept. Learning implies some modification to a behaviour; we then must remember that learning in order to retrieve and apply it.

Models of learning

Looking at the longer term, learning is a journey towards some kind of mastery – moving ultimately as close as possible to a comprehensive command of the understanding and skill required of the subject in question. But we need to look carefully at what learning looks like *in the short-term*. There are a number of models of learning; the following model is a well-known and reliable one which is represented by the journey from unconscious incompetence to unconscious competence:[27]

[27] Sometimes referred to as the Maslow Model (after American psychologist Abraham Maslow), it was in fact designed by management trainer Martin M. Broadwell in the 1960s.

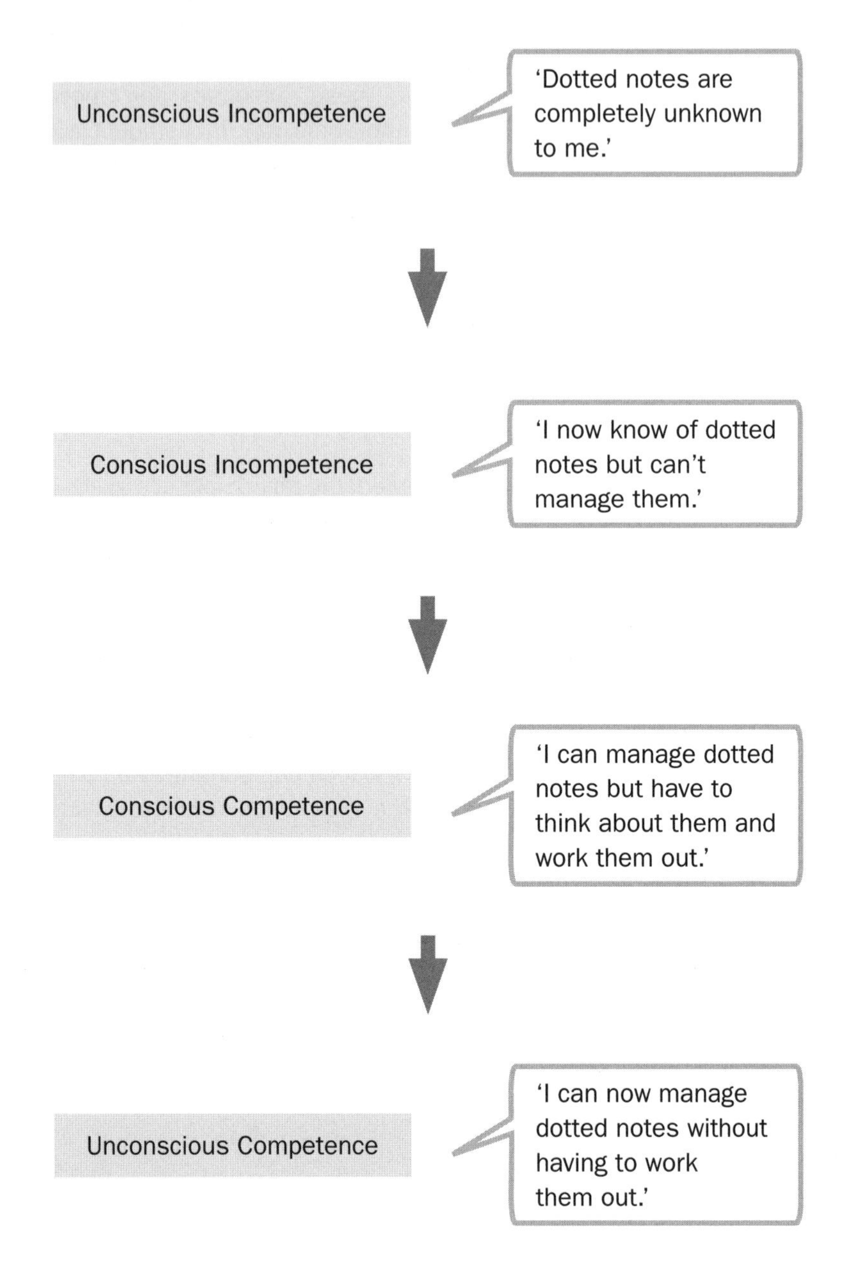

There is another model that I very much like. It is a rather simplified version of Meyer and Land's learning model that represents the journey like this:[28]

[28] The full description can be found here: Meyer, J.H.F. and Land, R., 'Threshold concepts and troublesome knowledge: Issues of liminality' in *Overcoming Barriers to Student Understanding: Threshold Concepts and Troublesome Knowledge* (Routledge, 2006).

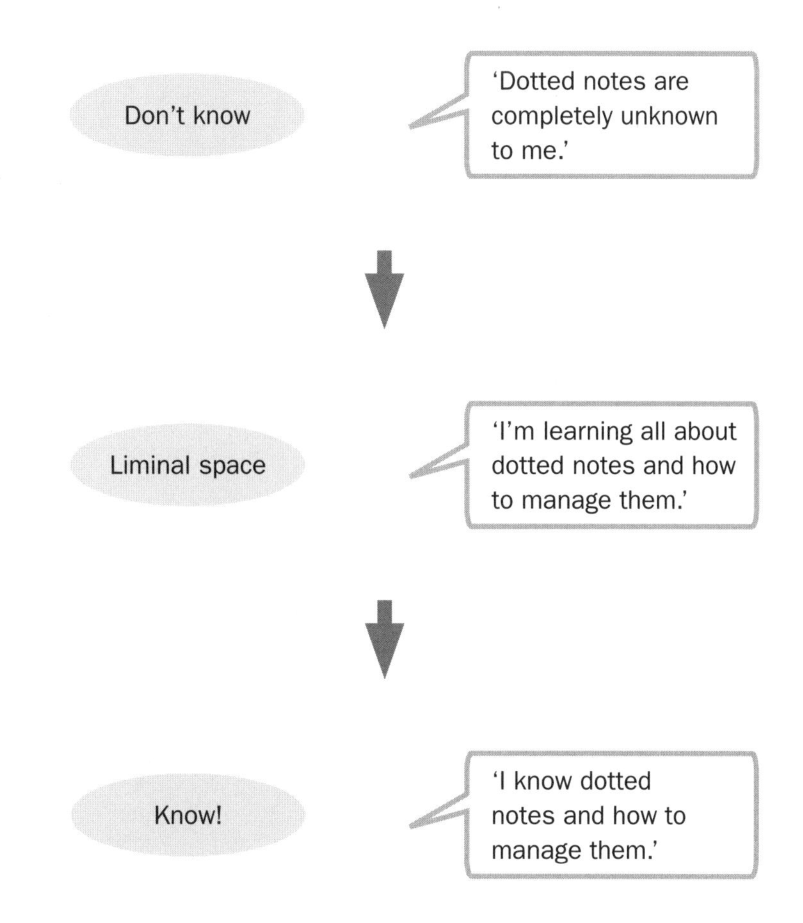

I teach this one to my students, too! They enjoy being able to express the success of their learning in this way: 'No, I'm still in liminal space with that!' they often say with a smile. Liminal space is a kind of in-between place – between not knowing and knowing. It's often much easier (and more fun) for students to say that something is in liminal space rather than 'I can't do this' or 'I haven't learned this,' or 'I've forgotten how to' or 'I didn't understand in the first place.' It reduces the potential for them feeling shame, guilt or anxiety if they think they should be able to do something and can't. Or maybe a student might be thinking: *My teacher thinks I can do it, but I can't and I feel ashamed to admit it.* This situation, which may block further learning, is removed.

To help and encourage the journey through liminal space into knowing there are certain principles we can follow. Using the Simultaneous Learning approach, in particular teaching through the ingredients and making clear, logical and understandable connections, will help our students see the bigger picture and how it all begins to fit together. If our style of teaching causes our student to *like* what they are learning, to see its need and relevance and therefore to *want* to learn it and see its place in the wider scheme of things, then reaching that goal of knowing is still more achievable.

To help, it's very important that we are thorough and explicit about our explanations; that we are clear why we're making a particular connection, that we often make the connection in collaboration with our student and we ask questions as we go along.

Let's take, for example, the teaching of scales – not everyone's favourite area of learning! To encourage success, ideally we need our students to:

- understand what scales are, what they are for and why it's helpful to learn them (through introducing appropriate **information**: background, theory and vocabulary);
- know how to play them (through developing appropriate technical **skills**);
- enjoy playing them (helping students to form a positive **attitude** towards them).[29]

[29] This is based on the three cornerstones of learning first written about by the American educational psychologist, Benjamin Bloom (Bloom's Taxonomy) and since then further developed by many other educationalists.

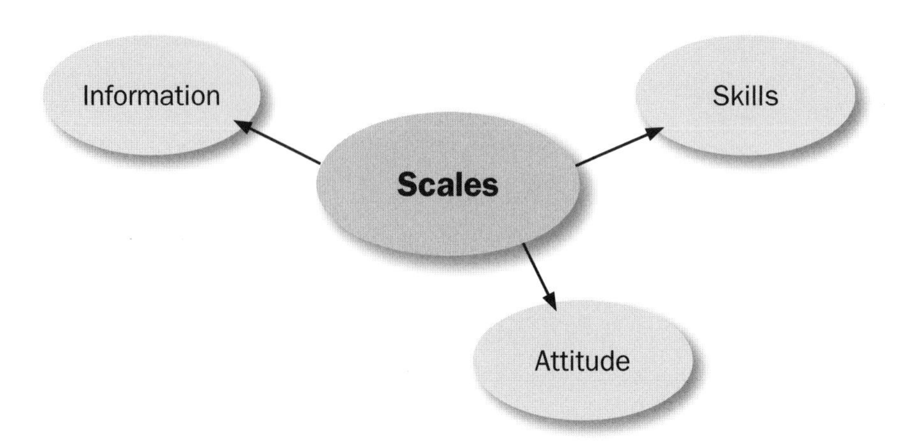

Teachers will have their own ways to accomplish these three areas (information, skills and attitude) but all three need to be considered and connected.

Asking questions is one of the best ways to help students consider scales in a more musical context and to help them begin to make connections and build up, cumulatively, that complete picture for themselves.

For example, if a student is learning a piece in G major along with the related scale, there are some questions to consider; by asking these questions over a period of time the three areas of gathering information, building skills and developing attitude will all be embraced.

1. Questions for **information** gathering:
   - Do you understand the key signature and what it signifies?
   - Do you understand tones and semitones and how that knowledge helps understanding and playing this scale correctly?
   - How many scale patterns can you find in your piece?
   - Can you see the scale patterns in this sight-reading piece?
   - What is similar (rather than different) about G major and (any other) major scale that you know?

2. Questions for **skill** building:
   - Which finger pattern will you be using? Why?
   - Are there any finger exercises you could create to help?
   - How is this scale going to help you play this piece?
   - Can you hear the scale in your head?
   - Can you imagine (hear) the scale in your head as you're playing it?
   - In your scale improvisation (improvising a short piece using the notes of the scale) how many ingredients can you include from your piece?
   - How can you learn to play the scale faster?
   - How will you learn to memorise the scale?

3. Questions to develop **attitude**:
   - Can you see the advantage of learning scales?
   - Can you feel the sense of going up and coming down?
   - Can you play the scale with the same character as your piece?
   - Can you play the scale with ingredients from your piece?
   - How does playing the scale tongued/with separate bows/ staccato change the character?
   - How does it make you feel if you pause on the F sharp?
   - Can you feel a sense of returning home when you reach the final note?
   - What colour is G major?
   - Does this scale have a particular character?

After a while students will really begin to 'get' the scale and see how it fits into the world of music. They will begin to know it – and know that they know it. And so, they will be able to apply their knowledge to other scales.

If we have taught in such a way that our students begin to feel that they can retrieve knowledge and manage skills easily, that they can apply what they know in different situations, and that they can, themselves, begin to make connections, then we have enabled them to develop their own musicality and capacity to learn more independently. More important still, they know these things are moving out of liminal space and into that knowing space. And more important still than that, when the time comes, they *know* that they know – which builds confidence and is very motivating. We can now enjoy the fact that the teaching really has been effective. We have given ourselves and our students control over the bigger picture – over knowing *about* knowing. Our student's awareness of their own learning and effort is now much greater.

This condition: *'I'll teach you on the condition that you're learning'* then ceases to be one. Because we are managing it. The benefit to both teacher and student is inestimable.

8 Group teaching

We also need to consider what it might look like to move towards teaching more unconditionally when working with groups – a situation that is often found in school or higher education music departments.

Group teaching in most instances offers the teacher a fairly equal balance of imaginative opportunities and challenges.[30] Learners, inevitably, behave differently within a group dynamic and, if encouraged appropriately, can develop increasing responsibility for both their own learning and for the learning of their peers.

[30] I have written on group teaching in detail in *Group Teaching in Practice*, *The Virtuoso Teacher* and *Simultaneous Learning* (all Faber Music Ltd). This chapter looks at group teaching from a conditional perspective.

But for this to happen, potential conditions that might obstruct or frustrate the flow of a lesson need to be managed (or better still, eliminated).

Let's look at the conditions that might affect a group lesson. I sent a short questionnaire to a number of group instrumental teachers asking them to respond to this thought:

The lesson might flow more effectively if (or, on the condition that) ...

Here are their responses:

- 'The students are (as) evenly matched (as possible).'
- 'The teacher's attention can be fairly equally distributed among the group members.'
- 'Students are not continually comparing themselves with each other.'
- 'I have good materials to use.'
- 'The lessons are long enough.'
- 'Schools (or institutions) get involved in showcasing students' progress.'
- 'The teaching room is large enough.'
- 'The instruments are all working properly.'

Of course, many of the conditions we've already discussed apply equally in the group teaching environment. The more practical (**passive**) conditions (size of teaching room, state of instruments, for example) do need to be satisfied and hopefully the institution will be helpful and do their best. But let's have a look at those conditions (the **active** conditions) that specifically relate to the group teaching situation; those that we as teachers may be able to manage and that we may have some control over.

The condition we will look at next is possibly the most significant ...

... the students are (as) evenly matched (as possible)

Here we are most likely talking about students being matched in experience and brain processing speeds and given that these vary *considerably* from one person to another (and to further complicate matters, individuals process different musical ingredients at different speeds), it's going to be inevitable that a group *won't* be evenly matched – or stay matched after the first few lessons. So, realistically, if a teacher's thoughts are *anywhere* on the following continuum (even at the extreme right-hand end) it will remain a condition and will potentially block the flow:

Thus, it is necessary to develop an approach to group teaching that accepts there will be a disparity in processing speeds – that students won't be matched ... *and that it doesn't matter.*

The group teacher needs to determine, early on in working with a new group, the strengths (and weaknesses) of each member of the group. These thoughts are always kept private but will help the teacher to encourage each member of the group to share their strengths with the others as each lesson unfolds. Those strengths could be connected with aspects of posture, technique, pulse, rhythm, sound, phrasing, theory, notation, leadership-like qualities, powers of imagination, use of descriptive language, and more. The beauty of group teaching is that the teacher doesn't need to be the lead figure all the time. Each member of the group can be encouraged to lead on aspects at which they feel confident – and there *will* be such opportunities for each member of the group in every lesson. Once the group gets into this kind of flow, much of the lesson can be directed in this way. Students will gain in confidence and learn effectively from each other.

Each student will get to know, understand, share their strengths and, interestingly, may well develop other aspects more quickly and readily in the group environment through watching and learning from their peers.

Whilst teaching in this (inevitably) mixed-ability environment will take a fair amount of thought and preparation, the results can be very effective.

Another related condition mentioned was *'I'm allowed to organise and choose which particular students make up each group rather than being allocated them by the school.'* If this can happen, it's both sensible and practical. The closer students are matched, at the earlier stages anyway, the smoother the journey forward will be.

Consequently, given this kind of approach, we remove students needing to be evenly matched as a condition.

... the teacher's attention can be fairly equally distributed among the group members

If the teaching follows the aforementioned approach, then this condition is unlikely to arise. There will be no place for the least effective style of group teaching, where the teacher seemingly deals with one student at a time (in reality giving each student a short individual lesson) or maybe prioritises one student because they are considered, for example, more innately musical. Instead, all students will be constantly engaged – playing, listening, thinking, contributing or indeed leading part of the lesson. In fact, students playing on their own will be a reasonably rare occurrence in an effective group lesson. Occasionally the teacher may have to spend time with an individual student, but the others, through their experience of this style of learning, will know how to make best use of the time working efficiently and productively with one another.

... students are not continually comparing themselves with each other

Learners will inevitably compare themselves with their peers.[31] They are surrounded by other students probably of very similar age and doing the same thing – it *is* inevitable. And most learners desire to know where they are in the pecking order. We have already considered ways to help students understand that whilst **self-comparison** is good, comparison with others is not helpful.[32] It's very much up to the teacher to remind their students regularly that if they are doing their best, that is, in itself, as good as it can be. Remind them also that one student is not *better* than another. All will have their particular strengths (and they will often be different strengths); one may be more advanced than another in a particular area, but we teach them to share and respect each other.

[31] Sometimes this might arise from existing family dynamics (sibling rivalries or maybe favouritism). We don't need to know the details, but it could be useful to bear them in mind.

[32] See Chapter 4, page 20.

A friendly level of competition where each student can probably 'win' at some time is of course perfectly acceptable. Personal bests are a fun addition to any lesson (and can become an important motivational part of practice, too). *Who can play the longest note? Who can keep their bow straightest? Who can play this passage the loudest or softest? Who can make the most effective diminuendo?*

Taking these thoughts into account, the condition can be managed and may even disappear.

... I have good materials to use

Having good materials and using them skilfully is clearly important and so it is not really a condition (or requirement) needing any validation or consideration. Nevertheless, it does seem worthwhile spending a moment considering materials in this context.

Group teaching is, in many ways, a different art compared with individual teaching – it's not simply like giving an individual lesson but to a number of students simultaneously. And the materials used play a *significant* part and do need to be chosen well.

In our effort to create an environment where working together is central to the success of the teaching and learning in the group situation, choosing effective *ensemble pieces* is particularly significant, and ensemble playing should form quite a portion of most, if not all, lessons. Ideally choose mixed-ability ensemble pieces where the parts offer each member of the group both security and just a little challenge. You may like to add or edit parts to make them more suitable. Encourage students to help each other as much and as often as possible. Swap parts (good for morale and equal opportunities) when you feel it would be safe to do so. Spend quite a proportion of each lesson on such work; students will learn a lot. And try to have a lot of varied and mixed ability ensemble repertoire available too, if possible.

... the lessons are long enough

Of course, it's helpful in every way if the lesson is sufficiently long enough to do all we would like to do. But if the lesson isn't, we have a choice: we can allow the limited time to be (and probably remain) a frustration, which will almost certainly, in some way, affect the value of what we do, or we can try to put that frustration to one side and make best use of the time. That's not to say that we shouldn't make every effort to negotiate for more time in whatever way we can, of course we should. But somehow, we need to see that as a separate issue.[33]

So, in the time we do have, use it all to teach in the manner described above, keeping all students as fully engaged as possible and always trying to encourage positive practice.

... schools (or institutions) get more involved in showcasing students' progress

This condition is well expressed in one response I received:

> 'There is a school I visit where the music teacher has encouraged all the class teachers to let the musicians perform to their class on a Friday afternoon (this extends to all musicians who would like to perform and not just the 'stars'). This has had a profound effect on the motivation of all my students: everyone has enjoyed hearing them and the students themselves have very much enjoyed sharing their music. I only ask students who are ready and confident to do this – but that's most of them!'

In addition, if schools can be encouraged to have ensembles, or even orchestras of some kind, in which students can play as soon as possible after starting lessons, it puts their learning into a very special and desirable context.

⁂

Assuming we take the considerations outlined into account and treat all members of any group as equally worthy (or unconditionally), we are well on the way to managing any condition that might get in the way and block the flow of effective teaching and learning in the group teaching environment.

[33] Moving towards a more unconditional approach doesn't mean that we should ever accept poor working conditions or being treated with anything other than the greatest of respect by those for whom we may be working. We must tackle these concerns or find someone to deal with them on our behalf but we do need to manage them in the shorter term, in such ways that stops them from blocking the flow of our teaching.

9 Do learners have conditions?

Whilst conditions are very much part of most *teachers'* lives, what about learners? And does age make a difference? Is there a significant difference in approach between school-age learners compared with adult learners?

I sent a short questionnaire to a number of learners in both the school-age and adult groups asking them to consider whether they do have conditions and how these might affect their experience as learners.

On the whole, it became clear, maybe a little surprisingly, that the responses from both groups were quite similar. In general educational terms there are clearly many differences between school-age and adult learners: the motivations behind and reasons for their learning; how members of the two groups actually go about their learning; their background experience; and, in certain ways, how we, as teachers, relate to the two groups on a more personal level.[34]

However, in answer to my questionnaire asking whether learners have any basic conditions and whether they have any conditions to satisfy in order to:

- practise more efficiently;
- work harder;
- enjoy the lessons more ...

... the various answers were not dissimilar – and certainly not sufficiently contrasted in any way to make the approach to students in these two age groups significantly different.

Also, it seemed to me that rather than 'conditions', the respondents thought more in terms of expectations or preferences but which, in this context, we might still define as conditions. In other words, they expect (and in many instances, prefer) their teachers to behave in certain ways. How much these will affect the flow and success of the teaching is certainly something for teachers to consider. The following are some (verbatim) replies from my survey:

Do I have conditions as a learner?

- 'Yes, I have to enjoy the learning process.'
- 'I'm not sure it's a condition, but I enjoy learning more if I'm able to go back to earlier pieces I've learned, and sense that I'm able to play them better.'
- 'I'll learn a new piece if my teacher is happy to play it through and send me a recording.'[35]

[34] I was interested to discover that the appropriate, though not very well-known, term for the world of adult education is 'andragogy', from the Greek meaning 'leading man'. 'Pedagogy' literally means 'leading children'. Malcolm S. Knowles has written on the subject in *The Modern Practice of Adult Education: From Pedagogy to Andragogy* (Follett Pub. Co., 1980).

[35] I have mixed feelings about this particular point, since it may encourage a dependency on 'rote' learning instead of music reading. On the other hand, in many musical cultures, e.g., Indian classical music, fiddle music and pop music to name a few, rote learning is more the traditional and accepted practice.

I would practise more if (on condition that) ...

- 'I'm confident of making real progress.'
- 'The practice space was more private.'
- 'I'm having fun.'
- 'My teacher didn't expect me to do so much.'
- 'I can be curious and non-judgmental about my mistakes.'
- 'I'm playing new repertoire.'
- 'I enjoyed the lessons more.'
- 'I had a better instrument.'
- 'I liked what I was practising.'
- 'My teacher wasn't so sarcastic about my practice.'

I'll work harder if (on condition that) ...

- 'My teachers are enthusiastic and seem to enjoy what they are teaching.'
- 'My teachers are passionate about their subject.'
- 'My teacher explains why I'm to do something.'
- 'My teacher shows me respect.'
- 'I feel encouraged by my teacher.'
- 'I can see/hear progress being made.'
- 'The teacher cares and puts things in a positive light. One of my teachers says, "If you don't do this homework, you won't learn anything." That doesn't help me.'
- 'I like the book I'm working from.'
- 'My teacher seems experienced and knows what they are doing.'
- 'It doesn't matter how much I get done.'
- 'My teachers are kind and make me feel welcome.'
- 'The lessons are interactive.'
- 'My teachers don't tell me about their problems.'
- 'My teachers are organised.'
- 'I succeed in playing a piece really well.'
- 'I'm enjoying the pieces and know that I'll have the chance to perform.'
- 'My teacher is never condescending.'
- 'I have goals that stretch me but are achievable.'

Here's a particularly poignant reply that came with a telling example:

> 'I work harder on the condition that my teacher gives me clear and precise feedback. I played a passage that included a few bars of semiquavers: "The semiquavers weren't very even, try it again" was my teacher's instruction. It was not helpful at all and I felt anxious and uncertain about what to do next.'

And here's a condition that a number of students at music college level have articulated:

> 'I'll work harder if my teacher really pushes me and really tells me how it is. I don't mind being bullied and told off when I deserve it.'

I feel this particular condition is worthy of comment: our ultimate aim must be to teach self-responsibility, resourcefulness and independence, especially if our student has reached tertiary level and, in the case of this student, is probably intending to make music a career. This sort of condition seems to be misguided as the student is apparently transferring the responsibility to the teacher: 'It's my teacher's fault if I don't work hard enough.'

Responsible teachers will always do their best to be absolutely honest and tell their students 'how it is' in no uncertain terms. They will also encourage them to work as hard as possible, but not in a bullying kind of way. The teacher who resorts to intimidation of any sort is helping to sustain a kind of teaching that brings no credit to the art and so often results in students becoming psychologically damaged, not to mention presenting a negative role model.

I'll enjoy the lessons more if (on condition that) ...

- 'I like the music we're doing.'
- 'My teacher is consistent with the feedback given.'
- 'The teacher makes the lesson interesting and fun.'
- 'My teacher doesn't waste time teaching me things I already know.'
- 'There's a balance between playing through the pieces and covering theory work.'
- 'I am making progress.'
- 'I'm not made to feel uncomfortable when asked to play on my own in a group lesson.'
- 'There's a lightness of touch and humour even when things are difficult.'
- 'I get positive feedback.'
- 'I don't get told off for getting something wrong.'
- 'The room is warm.'
- 'I feel like I know what I'm doing.'

Another interesting response (from someone who had given up playing) suggests that too rigid an approach doesn't yield happy consequences:

'I would have enjoyed my lessons more if my piano teacher hadn't have had such a systematic and rigid approach. I was required to "pass" a piece or stage before being allowed to progress to the next one, which meant playing perfectly as though each short exercise or piece were being examined. Pauline Hall's *Waltz of the semitone snakes* is a piece that has remained with me, having spent so much time trying to play it perfectly. In the end, this removed the enjoyment of playing, and the whole experience of learning. I feel this approach affected my confidence as well as the speed I was able to progress – it took me over three years to reach Grade 1. Eventually I gave up; perhaps with a more positive approach the outcome would have been different ... '

Many of these comments have been considered elsewhere in this book. And many of them probably wouldn't even enter a student's mind if they were being taught in a more unconditional manner. But there is certainly much food for thought here. You might even wish to discuss these thoughts with your students.

Do parents have conditions?

Having looked at the potential conditions of learners, it is also useful to look at whether parents have conditions. On the whole parents don't seem to have conditions if they feel the teacher is trustworthy and is there to do a good job. A positive, usually unspoken but highly desirable condition for a parent is that their child enjoys the process, gets a lot out of it and ultimately is then able to contribute to the greater good.

Of course, some parents do have less helpful conditions, and we know them well! Here are two, not uncommon, conditions:

'I'll encourage and be happy to pay for lessons on the condition that my child passes exams and secondly, that my child practises.'

If we believe our pupil will be better off without exams or is getting a lot from the lessons without as much practice as the parent might like, then some discussion with the parent will probably be necessary. Always be reasonable in your logic, expectations and thinking. It's very difficult to disagree with a case made through clear, rational and practical thought. Similarly, if a more informed or musical parent begins to impose particular requirements they feel important ('You must teach my child this repertoire, or this technique, or this skill'), again have some discussion to determine the best way forward.

[36] For a fascinating insight into 'tiger' parenting, read *Battle Hymn of the Tiger Mother* by Amy Chua (Bloomsbury, 2011).

Occasionally, we may meet what some might refer to as a 'tiger' parent.[36] Such parents are often very demanding and come with many (often) unrealistic expectations – in other words they come armed with a lot of conditions. If you decide to take the pupil on, it must, ultimately, be on your terms. Discussion and a clear explanation describing how you feel the teaching and learning should move forward is, of course, essential. But, if necessary, be firm. If you meet unreasonable resistance, then it may be prudent to recommend the parent seeks a new teacher. Self-protection is paramount.

Having now begun to unpack the many conditions experienced by both teachers and students (and parents), and how they may affect our approach to teaching and towards our students (and you may well have identified even more), let us further investigate the strategies that may help us to move forward into a world where these conditions become more managed. A more inclusive world that may engender a style of teaching where there is more opportunity for development and flow – just as in an effective musical performance. An environment where we can aspire to be more unconditional in our approach.

10 Moving forward

We have now looked in some detail at modifying our mindsets in order to accommodate many of the possible conditions that may have a bearing on our teaching. Now, we'll consider the teaching itself. Not *what* we teach – that is entirely up to each individual teacher – but the *way* we teach what we teach, looking particularly at some practical strategies that might cause our teaching to be less conditional.

Given our particular subject (music, and more specifically, musical performance) we do have a specific agenda. We do need to teach the nuts and bolts of instrumental and singing **technique**, we do need to stimulate thoughts that will result in an ability to convey **artistry** and we do need to teach all the various aspects that we might put under the overall heading of **language** (notation and reading, theory and developing the musical ear).

Whilst we might have some clear ideas of the best ways to teach these things, it's very important, as we try to be less conditional, to become more open-minded, supple and adaptable in the way we teach.

Formulaic teaching

Some teachers rely on tried and tested formulas: 'This is how I teach – the good students get it and the bad students don't.' This sentiment hides a condition: *'I'll be happy to teach you on the condition that you're capable of learning from my methods and respond the way I would expect and like best.'*

However, in reality, flexibility, adaptability and imagination are key qualities in the quest for more unconditional teaching. Different students 'get' things in different ways. It's very important that we don't give approval only to those students who learn best as a result of our own favourite way of teaching something.

As teachers we need to be aware that whilst some students may 'get it' the way we usually like to teach it, others inevitably won't. And it's important we don't consider those others as necessarily slower, less able or less 'musical' students.

It may be that we have to insert more steps (or make more connections) in order to get from A to B.

> These As to Bs could represent anything from not playing a note staccato to playing it staccato, not shaping a phrase to shaping it, or not understanding some rhythm to understanding it. Literally moving from a state of not quite getting something (which could be anything, however small) to getting it. A and B are merely two points with a distance in between.

Each of these extra steps (these extra connections) forms its own A to B and so the student is still making progress – still getting from *an* A to *a* B. But we are now working with these students in *their* best way and at *their* speed of progress.[37]

[37] This is particularly relevant when teaching dyslexic students and others with specific educational needs.

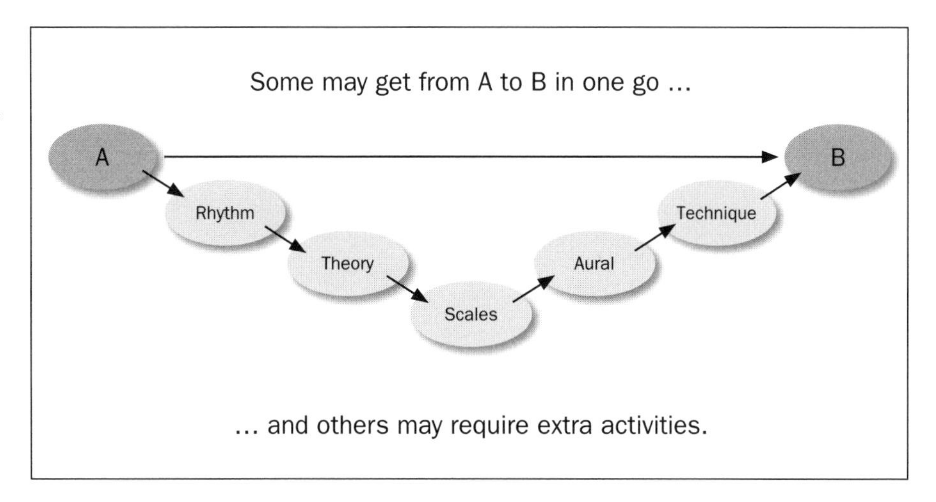

Teachers often have a particular series of steps that they've used time and time again to get from this particular A to B. But it may be that, for some students, we need to find a different order. Being flexible is at the heart of success.

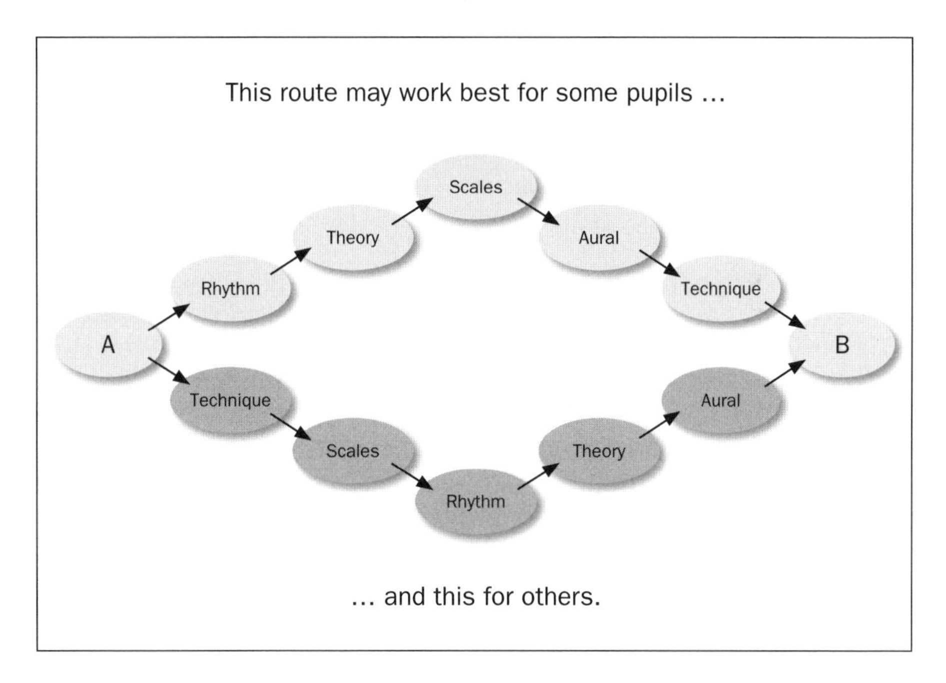

For some students it's not about inserting extra steps at all but finding the right route simply by supplying the one most apposite single connection. Maybe a student is not playing staccato lightly enough, for example. Many teachers will take the technical route but possibly the student will improve that staccato if they hear the appropriate sound internally (taking the aural route), maybe a little experimentation away from the piece in question (doing some improvisation), maybe they were playing too loudly (so experiment with dynamics), maybe they weren't thinking rhythmically enough or maybe an appropriate demonstration may help – the important thing is to ensure they understand what it is they are to do differently (in a non-condescending way):

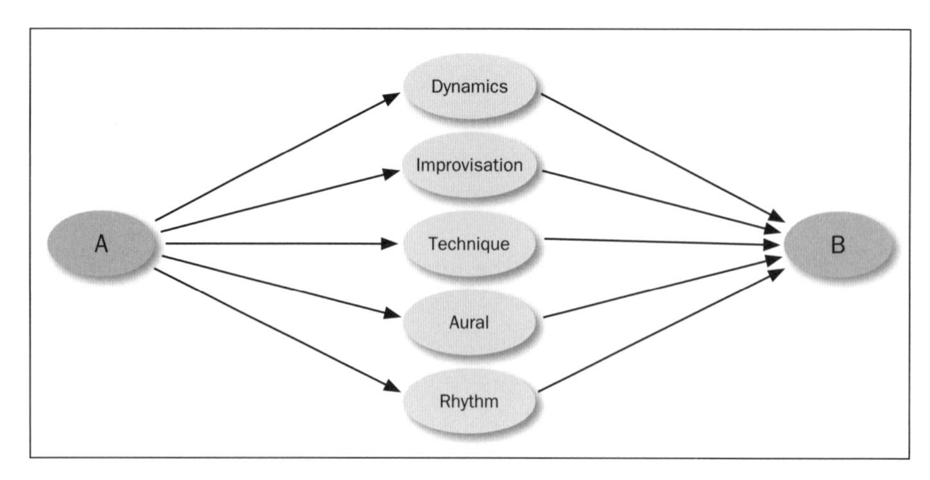

Some teachers have a fairly set routine for their lessons, for example:

1. Two minutes of warm-ups
2. A scale (not necessarily in the key of the piece later to be studied)
3. Two pieces to work on and maybe some sight-reading or aural training (if there is time or, for example, an exam is on the horizon)

Going through the lesson in this way becomes a kind of condition, and if things don't work as expected, there may be a degree of irritation. But whist routine can create a feeling of safety, learners may respond well to just a little occasional chaos![38] Just allow your imagination to get the better of you and let the energy of the lesson simply take you where it wants to ...

[38] Learners who may have Autism Spectrum Disorder often appreciate the routine of having their lessons at a set time on a set day but even they don't necessarily need lessons planned out or the activities delivered in a set order. After making connections with the previous lesson and any practice they may have done, they often latch onto an ingredient(s) and have their own preferred way of how they want the lesson to move forward.

Perhaps take the first note from a piece or phrase and set about exploring it:

How many different characters or different tonal colours can it be given?

▼

Can it be played fast or slow; talk about fast and slow, what do those words mean?

▼

Play something fast, play something slow; what are we actually doing when we play fast or slow?

▼

Find four notes to represent fast and four to represent slow, play some fast notes slowly and some slow notes 'fast' ...

It's not chaos really. It's just veering off the main road and slipping down a less well-known path – you just never know what you might find!

Simultaneous Learning and responding positively

I have written extensively on this approach to teaching.[39] Simultaneous Learning is all about encouraging a style of teaching that cultivates a deep understanding and a love for learning. The effectiveness of the *learning* is at its heart. When asked to describe it as concisely as possible, I simply list its three main principles:

[39] See *Simultaneous Learning* (Faber Music Ltd).

- Teach through the ingredients (of a piece or a song) which may include key, rhythm patterns, technical requirements, style, character and markings;
- Make explicit and clearly explained connections between all those ingredients, be they musical, technical or theoretical areas, that might contribute to a holistic understanding as you proceed;[40]
- Teach proactively: in other words, set up each activity (getting from A to B) carefully, logically and sequentially based on the student's response to the previous activity, in order to maximise the chances of success.

[40] All are set out in my *Simultaneous Learning Map of the Musical World* available to download from *paulharristeaching.co.uk*

Simply teaching in this way reduces (even eliminates) so many conditions. It liberates both teacher and student from the kind of unimaginative, compartmentalised teaching and the 'you play and then I'll react to your mistakes' (or 'your misunderstanding') kind of teaching, which is inevitably judgemental, non-collaborative and unlikely to produce independent musicians who can, ultimately, go away and do music on their own.

At the heart of this style of teaching is the ability to respond positively and constructively. Rarely (ideally, never) should a teacher respond negatively or destructively – both of which are toxic and will eventually cause most students to lose any resolve they may have had and ultimately give up. (I have also written on how we can achieve this style of response in *The Virtuoso Teacher.*[41]) Here I'd like to consider the *conditionality* of that response – its importance is critical. We might say that the success of our teaching is conditional on it!

[41] See Chapter 4, 'Getting the best out of our pupils' (Faber Music Ltd).

When thinking about conditionality, we need to consider to what extent the positivity of our response is conditional on how well our student carried out the activity. First of all, we need to be aware that our response will probably be delivered with both a verbal and non-verbal element. We should always aspire to respond with some encouraging words spoken in positive tones which we deliver with maybe a smile or a nod (or other positive body language), simultaneously being aware of the effect of that response on our student. It's very interesting and helpful to know that recipients of feedback are principally affected by our body language, which research tells us is processed in a fraction of a second.[42]

[42] It's also important to remember that those with Autism may be unable to read body language.

Of course, we should *always* try to respond to our students' efforts *positively*. Certainly, we don't need to praise when praise is not due, but the student has put themselves on the line by making an attempt, risking failure and rejection. This is a real achievement, and we must applaud them for that at the very least. **So, whatever our student did, it is always possible to find a positive and constructive response to move the lesson forward.**

It's also very important that there is a deeper message conveyed. It's human nature to like being liked and dislike being disliked. The message 'I still like you whatever the quality of your attempt' must somehow never be compromised. It is entirely normal to seek approval, appreciation, and acceptance by others, especially those in an authority position – in this case, the teacher. Any sense of rejection may endanger the positive direction of the lesson, and maybe, looking from a wider perspective, the future of that particular teacher-student relationship.

Moving positively from A to B

If the activity (getting from A to B) was set up in the logical and sequential manner in the tradition of Simultaneous Learning, then the chances are that it will have been successfully carried out and so a positive response would be absolutely appropriate. If the student 'nearly' got it then such a response would also be appropriate with some encouragement, along with some small refinements and suggestions before having another go.

If the activity was poorly carried out, we might have to consider that we may have been unintentionally responsible. It was possibly the wrong thing to have done at that particular moment. It happens – and we can still be positive in our general response and immediately go on to reset the activity. That's good teaching.

In general, the Simultaneous Learning teacher will almost always set up activities and challenges that can be met. Any oncoming technical aspects, for example, will have been dealt with beforehand – the student is rarely put in a position where they don't know what they are about to do. But occasionally a teacher may have made an assumption about a particular aspect of a student's specific ability and the student does slip up (or makes a genuine mistake). Even in this instance the response can be positive and there is no harm done.

Simultaneous Learning and practice

Let's look at how this might translate into our students' practice. Success is motivating. Students may (instinctively) rely on getting things right to motivate their practice. Getting things right makes us feel good – it releases endorphins, and so, like wanting another piece of chocolate (because *it* releases endorphins), it motivates us to do some more practice!

> *'I'll enjoy (and indeed will) practice on the condition that I get things right.'*

After all, no one enjoys getting things wrong. We need to teach our students to manage this condition. We need to help them put strategies into place that will reduce the number of times they might get things wrong.

To help my students practise positively and unconditionally I teach them what I call 'The Double-O Mindset'. It encourages them to be **O**bservational and **O**bjective. It is about **observing** carefully what has just been done and then reacting to it in an **objective** manner (just like we do in the teaching situation).

The observation is mostly aural – listening with real intent, but also being aware of physical aspects and how they may relate to what was heard.[43]

[43] Singers will have to use a slightly different approach as the sound they hear internally is not what others will hear externally. Recording their singing (using the best quality equipment they can) will make this approach possible.

In practising, if something doesn't quite work, the reaction is not 'why **can't** I do this?' expressed in a rather annoyed and frustrated manner, but rather, '**why** can't I do this?' expressed quietly and thoughtfully. Doing so opens up a route for a more objective, non-judgemental review without any negative thoughts or emotions wasting time and getting in the way.

We want to teach our students to avoid thinking negative thoughts like 'I did that badly' or 'that wasn't very good'. These are subjective, judgmental thoughts and simply waste time. Instead, much better to learn to think observationally and objectively:

'I didn't achieve quite what I wanted, maybe because I played …

… too loudly;
… not smoothly enough;
… with too much accent;
… not quite in tune;
… with the wrong bowing;
… with too much tension.'

And so on. The follow-up question is then: *what* am I doing (or what am I not doing) that is preventing me from achieving this particular goal.[44] 'What' questions are always objective and less emotional, and will often take you much closer to a solution much more quickly. And so to the next thought and action …

[44] Practice is really just an opportunity for the student to set up a series of appropriate goals for themselves and then find enjoyable and creative strategies to attain them. This is another step towards creating an independent musician.

'I'll try this instead …'

This response will be constructive, positive and move the practice forward in a good direction. Most importantly, students become more independent.

Thus taking real care over *our* responses to our students' work and encouraging our students to think more about *their* responses to their own work, the environment in which both teachers and students operate begins to become much more unconditional.

⁂

Moving towards unconditional teaching: a roadmap

Before we finally take a close look at ourselves and how we might best serve our teaching, here's a roadmap that summarises the journey we might make on this movement towards more unconditional teaching:

Think about your teaching space – can you make it more of a special place? Maybe bring a plant, a picture of the sun, or something beautiful or inspirational to the room.

↓

Make a list of any active conditions you feel may be getting in the way or blocking the flow and begin to think about ways to manage them more effectively.

↓

Make a mental note of how often your student smiles or clearly shows enjoyment.

↓

Begin to reduce the number of errors you mention and instead correct students (if they continue to make mistakes or slips) in more imaginative ways.

↓

Begin to move towards a more Simultaneous Learning approach.

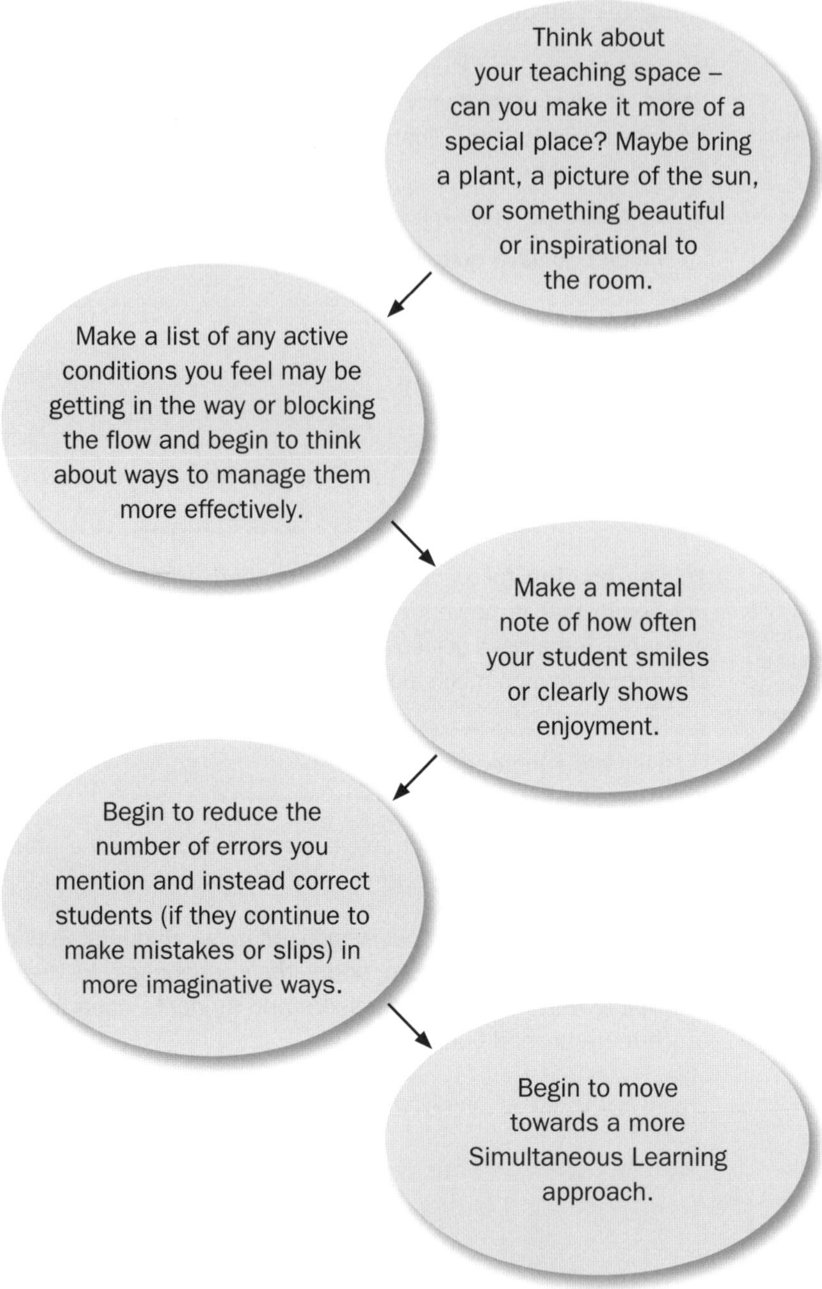

11 Looking inwards

Finally, we need to look inwards, maybe quite deeply inwards into our own personalities, to determine whether we are thinking in ways which can reduce – and perhaps even eliminate – some of our conditions.

There are three areas to consider: **self-awareness, empathy** and **ego**.

Self-awareness

First of all, we need to develop high levels of self-awareness. In particular, we need to be aware of what we say and do, and the effect this has on our students.

There are two main considerations here:

- Being aware of our deep values and beliefs and how they affect our behaviour and expectations.
- Being aware of how we are perceived by others.

High levels of self-awareness can lead to high levels of self-control (or self-containment)[45] – we begin to manage what we say and do more carefully. That's not to say that we can't be instinctive and spontaneous. And if we are balanced and self-aware in our approach, we can shift smoothly from instinctive and spontaneous responses to more intentionally considered ones when required in order to move forward positively. This behaviour derives from a deeper understanding about the consequences of our actions, and so we become more aware of our conditions.

[45] Which in particular means having control over one's actions, impulses, or emotions.

It also embraces what psychologists call mentalisation: our potential capacity to understand the deeper reasons that drive and underly our behaviour. More simply, it's the ability to know oneself intellectually, which can guide us to more informed choices and actions.[46]

[46] For further discussion on mentalisation you might like to try *Attachment in Psychotherapy* by David Wallin (Guilford Press, 2015).

We have, to some degree, already considered this when thinking about our more hidden conditions. Without getting too deeply involved in psychological matters, it is useful to self-observe (be aware of) our behaviour, recognise the effect it has on our students and respond accordingly.

Maintaining the flow

If a lesson is going along well, if both teacher and student are effortlessly engaged and each activity is developing logically and sequentially from the last, then there is nothing to concern us. Just maintain that flow – the positive energy (in both student and teacher) will be unmistakeable. But if things are not going so well, we need to recognise:

- if we have said something our student doesn't understand;

- if we have explained something in a way our student doesn't understand;
- if we have asked them to do something they're not sure how to do;
- if we have responded in such a way as to cause our student to be confused or distressed, or maybe to feel patronised ...

... and then be aware (and care about) exactly how we move forward.

For real success we give an instruction or explanation to our student, simultaneously (and instinctively) expecting that its probable effect will be a positive one. If we give an inappropriate instruction or deliver an explanation that doesn't quite work (not deliberately but maybe the result of a mistaken assumption) it needs fixing right away. The realisation that there may be a problem will be the result of carefully observing and being aware of our student's reaction. Our higher form of self-awareness will allow us to remain entirely in control when we do fix the problem. It will enable us to remain calm, positive and constructive. The problem will be fixed, maybe in the Simultaneous Learning way: in good spirit and either by inserting more micro-activities, possibly by making a different connection or by seeing a slightly different route forward.

This awareness gives us more control over *our* response and by understanding any preconceived conditions we may have, we are able to manage those conditions effectively during the lesson. We are beginning to teach unconditionally.

Coded negativity

Sometimes we may say something that on the surface seems innocuous enough but arises from a deeper frustration that we probably didn't mean to communicate – but nevertheless we do! And such a comment may have a greater consequence than we might imagine. A superficially positive comment might be received as a kind of coded negative message. Maybe the lesson begins with a reasonable question: 'Have you had much time for practice this week?' (teacher assuming that, as usual, this student often hasn't) and we ask the question with an almost imperceptible (and probably unintentional) negativity in the inflection. This could so easily be interpreted as a veiled criticism and the lesson gets off to a poor start in the mind of the student.

Sometimes a teacher may make such a comment intentionally. This, however, can be regarded as being manipulative and should be avoided. Students may end up feeling guilty (as the teacher probably intended) or interpret it for what it is was and so begin to dislike the teacher.

Empathy

Can we actually know what effect we might be having on our students? Understanding any potential impact on our students is part of what many psychologists call Emotional Intelligence. Empathy is part of our Emotional Intelligence and is very much concerned with our ability to feel what another person feels (by being receptive and intuitive) so we can communicate more successfully. In particular it will take into account how the other person (in this case our student) is *thinking and feeling* about:

- What they are doing
- What we are teaching them
- How the lesson is going

Strictly speaking, empathy is usually something we can demonstrate to someone who may be experiencing difficulties that are (usually) *not* of our making. However, in the teaching situation we are referring to the reactions that inevitably *are* the result of our making. Empathy in this context means the teacher is able to react immediately and effectively to their students' responses.

Without getting too immersed in the various types of empathy,[47] as teachers, we need to be strongly aware if we do lose our students' focus, attention and concentration; or if they are feeling uneasy or troubled by something we may have asked them to do. Changes in energy levels, tone of voice and facial expression can all be indicators of how our students are getting on. The quicker we can pick up the signals the quicker we can put things right and get back into the flow.

Thus, through empathy we can become still more aware of our conditions and therefore more able to control them.

Ego

Finally, to what degree are we conditioned by our egos? This prompts the ultimate question: why am I teaching? It's a simple fact that for most of us, we teach because it's what we do and we do it to make a living. Beyond this, what are the underlying reasons why we teach? These reasons cover a broad spectrum and should certainly go a lot further than to get the student onto the next page in the book or the next item on the exam syllabus.

On one hand, the answer is we teach because we, each in our own way, *really* can make the world a better place in which to be. Maybe only slightly better, but certainly better, nonetheless. As teachers we are helping others to achieve and to discover their best selves – to help them build and develop their sense of self-worth. And as music teachers there is the added dimension that we are passing on our love of this highest of creative art forms and playing a part in sustaining its future. Consequently, we are contributing something deeply worthwhile and uniquely important to society. That is a good place to be.

On the other and less attractive end of that spectrum are those who may be teaching to feed their egos, their sense of superiority and self-importance. The kind of teacher who only wishes to teach 'the most talented' and who possesses a sense of entitlement which will probably negatively influence the overall reach of their work and may often lead to their own disappointment, frustration and unhappiness. And possibly to treating their apparently 'less capable' students with a certain degree of contempt. Their aim in teaching is

[47] Currently, psychologists list five types of empathy: cognitive, emotional, compassionate, somatic (relating to the body) and spiritual. There are many good books on the subject – if you'd like to explore this further try: *Empathy: Why It Matters, And How To Get It* by Roman Krznaric (Rider, 2015).

to create students very much in their own image – an aspiration that, in many cases, is destined to fail. That is not a good place to be. The closer a teacher is to this end of the spectrum, the more conditional they are.

The approach of those on one end of the spectrum can be characterised as 'I'll teach anyone who wants to learn, irrespective of conditions' while those at the opposite end of the spectrum think: 'I'll only teach (the tiny minority) who satisfy all of my (many) conditions.' Those teachers, constrained by all these conditions, are inevitably going to be very hard to please.

Some may argue that if we are highly conditional (in that our expectations are always excessively high) and maybe also slightly impatient, it's more likely to encourage higher levels of attainment, and more likely to create an environment in which students can develop more advanced technical and musical skills.

Being more unconditional doesn't compromise quality or excellence. But it does allow us to do our best for *all* our students – something that is especially important in the times in which we presently live. We can have quality and excellence at any level, and for each and every student who wants to learn. So let's aspire to recognising and then reducing those more negative conditions to enable the greatest number of our students to achieve. And by reducing, perhaps even eliminating those conditions, we can substantially increase the extent of their achievement. Enlarging the base of the pyramid will ultimately make that pyramid both stronger and higher.

Being kind to ourselves

It is also important to turn the tables and consider that we have to be unconditional towards ourselves, too. In our quest to be and do the best we can, we must take care to remember that we are human. Whilst of course we strive, always, to be and do the best we can, we must allow for the fact that we don't always have limitless energy and our imaginations might not always be firing on all cylinders; we might occasionally be feeling down, and we will inevitably sometimes get things wrong. It's important that we accept these limitations if they occur and not allow them to cause us stress. *Occasionally, lessons given at a little lower than our usual delivery level is quite acceptable*, which potentially allows our students to see that we're neither perfect nor indestructible, therefore giving them permission to accept their own limitations.

> Furthermore, it's important to consider that by imposing conditions on our students we are also, in a way, imposing those conditions on ourselves.

Towards unconditional teaching

You may recall the statement that opened Chapter 2:

It is a poetic statement. Also a true one. The sun *is* unconditional. The sun's light and warmth affect us all, unconditionally. But it isn't an entirely ideal parallel with our role as teachers. The sun is an inanimate body and has no choice but to be unconditional. Human beings are continually making choices and are much more complex in their conditionality.

But with increased awareness we can all aspire to be more unconditional in our teaching, which benefits the teacher as much as the student. Personal satisfaction of the teacher is absolutely central to a more unconditional approach.

We can probably never be *absolutely* unconditional (nor should we be) – but if we see the advantages of more unconditional teaching, and we see the journey as on a continuum, it gives us the chance to flow gently in the direction of more unconditional teaching without feeling we have to make any sudden or sweeping changes in our approach:

Conditional teaching ⟵⟶ Unconditional teaching

Unconditional teaching is not an outcome or a destination that at some point we finally reach; much better to think of it as a state towards which we should always be striving. As a result, it can have a powerful and transformative effect on the success of our teaching and on the future of our students. And maybe even on the future, in a much broader sense.

It does seem something well worth aspiring to.

You may also recall that we began (a little paradoxically) by listing certain (positive) conditions that constitute a strong foundation on which the very best teaching is built. So, let's also end (a little paradoxically) with a condition ...

There is a magical *space in the middle* during a lesson. It's a bit like the indefinable space that exists between the performer and the audience when all parties are wholly focussed and effortlessly engaged, or between some great acting and an especially receptive and entranced audience. On the joint conditions that the teacher, through being as unconditional as possible, is in the flow and the student mirrors that flow, then that *space in the middle*, that unconditional space, between teacher and student can become truly energised and magic takes place.

The most powerful teaching and learning is happening.